A Love for
the Lost

CW01091502

A Love for the Lost

David Brainerd

Brian H. Cosby

CF4•K

10 9 8 7 6 5 4 3 2

Copyright © 2011 Brian H. Cosby

Paperback ISBN: 978-1-84550-695-7

epub ISBN: 978-1-84550-875-3

mobi ISBN: 978-1-84550-876-0

Reprinted 2014

Published by
Christian Focus Publications,
Geanies House, Fearn, Ross-shire,
IV20 1TW, Scotland, U.K.

Tel: +44 (0)1862 871011
Fax: +44 (0)1862 871699
www.christianfocus.com
email: info@christianfocus.com

Cover design by Daniel van Straaten
Cover illustration by Brent Donoho
Printed and bound in Denmark by Nørhaven

Scripture quotations are based on the King James Version
of the Bible.

Contents

To Ashley,
a selfless woman, a loving mother,
and my faithful wife.

Mystery in the Making
August 1737

David bolted up the muddy path leading to his home, almost skipping with excitement. As the sunlight danced on the ground through the waving branches from the large oak trees lining the path, he tried to only run in the shadows as if he were playing a game with the trees.

An afternoon thunderstorm had blown through an hour before and David's wet clothes suctioned around his body, although he couldn't tell if it was more from the rain or his sweat. Either way, he didn't care. He was finished for the day and enjoyed the thought of kicking his feet up and reading a book down at the public library.

As David got closer to his house, he began to feel out of breath and eventually slowed to a shuffle; where his feet didn't leave the ground at all. All of a sudden, he felt a sharp pain in his side and bent over. "Just a stitch," he thought to himself, trying to take a couple of deep breaths, his throat burning a little.

Like every young man his age, he loved working hard and getting dirty. It made the cool water of the washbasin so much more refreshing! He stood up and looked at his calloused hands, remembering how the plowing had taken a toll on them earlier in the springtime. At once, he felt like an old man – with years of living, and growing and farming. He looked up the path toward his home and smiled. "But I am not that old yet!" He sprinted the rest of the way, up the front steps and barged through the open doorway. "Home!"

Summers in Durham, Connecticut—as in most of southern New England—were generally hot and humid and the afternoons occasionally brought a thunderstorm. There was nothing really special about Durham except that it was home to one of the first public libraries in America, called "The Book Company of Durham," established only four years earlier in 1733. Many of the original books of the library were donated by the Rev. Nathaniel Chauncey, Jr, who had inherited his father's religious and theological book collection. Settlers first arrived in Durham in 1699, which at that time was a hunting area used by the Mattabesset Indian tribe. They called the land Coginchaug, which meant "long swamp" because much of the area was swampy and low-lying—a perfect kind of place for mosquitoes!

David had inherited the Durham farm from his family a few months earlier and was hoping to really enjoy the work. He grew up in a town called Haddam, located ten miles east of Durham and where most of his family still lived. It was only a few months earlier that he began tilling the ground and planting corn and all sorts of vegetables. The Coginchaug River provided Durham's farmlands with adequate water and the children a constant source of summer swimming!

That afternoon, the sun peeked over the nearby Metacomet Ridge, creating an orange glow throughout town. After David changed clothes, he grabbed some ink, a quill, and some paper and walked out the door toward the library. The library was actually in the home of one of Rev. Chauncey's relatives, Nathan Chauncey, and only people who lived in Durham could become members.

Tilling the ground, removing rocks and planting vegetables caused David to reconsider a life of farming. "I do not believe I can do another summer here!" he thought to himself as turned down Fowler Avenue. "I feel like I was created for more than this. But what? Maybe a trade business up and down the river to Boston."

As he made his way along, he came to a spot on the road where he could see the river below and suddenly saw a group of Indians fishing. He stopped and just looked, amazed by their simplicity and ... their *otherness*.

There wasn't anything new about seeing Indians, but he was nevertheless intrigued. Growing up, David had always heard about them and would even see them from time to time in Haddam; usually trading food or furs for metal tools. But every time he saw one, he wanted to know more about them.

As the English moved further westward, deeper into the heart of America, they would often come into contact with various Indian tribes. Some of the Indians were interested and cordial; and some were not. Too often, the result of the westward expansion by the English brought conflict, disease, killing and new landowners.

You would have thought the Indians were part-animal by the way the people of New England talked about them sometimes. They were known as "savages" or "heathens". While many labeled them and saw them as lower class, David had compassion on them. They were fellow human beings who needed the gospel of Jesus Christ, just as much as any man or woman, boy or girl.

Still watching from the road, David thought about whether or not they knew Jesus. "They probably do not attend church anywhere," he thought to himself. "I wonder if they have ever even heard of Jesus before." Though David had always attended church as a boy, he hadn't really felt a deep love for God before—like he heard about from other people.

During the early to mid-eighteenth century, just about everyone went to church. In fact, much of life centered around involvement with the local church and conversing with the local minister. People talked about the sermon throughout the week and would use the Westminster Confession of Faith to catechize their children. David had been catechized a little, usually by his older brothers. It was a simple question and answer study tool that described the basics of the Christian faith. To David, learning his catechism was more of a duty and chore than anything, though at times he liked learning the definitions of big words—"justification," "sanctification" and the like.

As he stood on the bank of the river, enjoying the shade from a large oak tree, he continued to watch his Indian friends. Some used blowguns while others used a series of nets that seemed to trap the fish in a confined area. The Indians were excellent hunters, fishermen and farmers. Although they hadn't learned some of the latest techniques of the trade in Europe, they had inherited centuries of hunting and farming wisdom passed down from their ancestors. It was not uncommon for them to teach the "white man" how to grow various crops in the New England climate.

David couldn't help thinking of his farm. All farming seemed to do was take away from him his time reading, which he considered a great privilege and joy. In a time when not everyone could read and books were quite expensive, David found that his affection and interest in all sorts of subjects grew and deepened through reading. So when the new library was set up in Durham, he was eager to move there even though he had to work the farm.

Among the many subjects he enjoyed reading about—including adventure stories—he really enjoyed learning about the English Puritans and the great Reformers of Europe, like Luther and Calvin, who had broken away from the Roman Catholic Church two hundred years earlier. Though he didn't feel a strong love for God in his heart, he, nevertheless, took interest in theology and church history.

David took issue at times with Calvin's teachings on predestination, though he knew that Scripture clearly taught it. Nevertheless, he studied and read all about God's electing love. Rev. Chauncey, the library's donor, was a Calvinist, which meant that (among other things) he believed that God was in control over all things, including a person's eternal salvation. God chose his people even before the creation of the world—the "elect"—as the Bible calls them.

The study of God and the Bible intrigued David, but it remained nothing more than simple intrigue. His heart was often turned off godly things and he even doubted if he really believed that Jesus was his Savior and Lord. However, he was grieved when people claimed to be a Christian and lived such awful and openly sinful lives.

By this point, the Indians were beginning to count their catch and David figured he probably better get on toward the library. He continued down Fowler Avenue until he reached the rather large two-story house.

"Good day, Mr. Brainerd," greeted a tall gentleman, tipping his dark hat a bit.

David looked up. "Good afternoon, sir."

He walked in and, quickly finding a book, sat down in a large oak chair in the corner of one of the rooms. "Mr Calvin's Institutes of the Christian Religion," he read softly, opening the cover. He flipped to Book Two, which concerns the revelation of Jesus Christ, and began to read. But for some reason he couldn't concentrate. His mind began to re-trace his childhood and how he got to where he was—in an oak chair, reading Calvin's Institutes and working a farm in Durham.

David was born the sixth child and third son of his parents, Hezekiah and Dorothy Brainerd on Sunday, April 20th, 1718. Like his brothers and sisters, he had his fair share of chores around the family farm and home, but also enjoyed fishing, swimming and ice-skating in the winter. His education was done through his parents who taught him in history, Latin, grammar, reading, math and, of course, catechism.

Morning and evening, his father would lead the family in devotions and worship, which included either talking about the previous week's sermon or explaining a particular passage of Scripture. The worship would also include singing hymns together. Being that both of his grandfathers were officers in the local church in Haddam obviously dictated his regular and punctual attendance at church each week. The church of that day did not have lights or a fire to keep it warm in the wintertime and it wasn't uncommon for sermons to extend nearly two hours in length. But church life was part and parcel of eighteenth-century New England life.

Though he had a rather large family, he didn't have many friends. In fact, he often felt lonely and depressed—not taking the initiative to get to know boys his age. When he was only nine years old, his father got sick and died suddenly. In the years that followed, David had to pick up extra duties around the home, such as tilling the land, harvesting crops, and repairing the house. Four years later—just before his fourteenth birthday—his mother also passed away. Orphaned from that day, he had been living with different family members and he felt like a nomad, with no true home.

As he sat in his chair, daydreaming back to his childhood life, his mind began to shift to thinking about the Indians he had seen that day. For some reason, he wanted to know if they had heard of Jesus. "What would I tell them anyway?" he whispered to himself. "What if they asked me about the Bible? I don't really know it at all." While he had studied the Bible in pieces, he had never taken serious time to actually read it all the way through. That, however, was about to change.

The summer faded into fall and the fall into winter. Though he didn't know it at the time, David's life would take him on a wild adventure into the mysterious plan and purpose of God. And perhaps, too, God would even draw David into a close relationship through suffering and hardship. It is, no doubt, how he often works.

Hazed and Confused
December 1738

"Finished!" Brainerd yelped, slamming the book down on the kitchen table. He couldn't believe he'd actually read it again!

"Would you keep it down in there?" called an older gentleman from the nearby bedroom.

David shot up. "Oh, yes, yes, sir, Pastor Fiske. I'm sorry." He glanced around the living area and the small kitchenette and noticed the white kettle sitting on the wood-burning stove. "Would you like your evening tea, sir?"

The old pastor appeared from around the bedroom door and smiled, rubbing his glasses with his shirt. "What did you finish, my boy?"

"The Holy Bible, Reverend," he said with a grin. He looked back down at the old book sitting on the table. "It is the second time this year I have read it wholly through."

"Good!" Fiske said with a cheerful surprise. "Has it had effect on you?" He paused for a second and peered through the lenses as if inspecting them for smudges and then looked at David.

David was confused. "Effect?"

"Are you a better man for reading it, young lad?"

"Better?" he thought to himself. He picked the Bible up and rubbed the leather cover with his fingers.

"I am not sure. It is a good thing to read the Bible, right? I mean, I am a better person because I read the Bible." He began to speak louder and louder. "You know, sir, not many people read the Bible and I have now read it twice this year alone!"

"Did reading it teach you anything about humility?" the Pastor asked, putting his glasses on.

"Well, yes. I am quite humble I would say."

Fiske took a deep breath and returned to his bedroom shaking his head.

David looked back down at the Bible. "Doesn't God accept me more because I have read his Word? Twice now?" He peered at the Reverend's bedroom door. "And what did the Pastor mean by learning humility? I am humble!" he thought to himself.

The next day, David rose early in the morning, bundled up, and, after spending some time reading Genesis, set out to buy some bread and venison. Passing down a row of houses, he overheard some middle-aged men talking rather seriously from inside one of the houses. He couldn't quite make out what they were saying, but it was something about how Fiske's sermons were too long and uninteresting. David was amazed at the carelessness of others with regard to spiritual things. He wondered if they had ever even read the Bible at all.

The winter months in Haddam were strikingly different from the summer and often relentless. Drifts of snow blanketed the sides of houses and ice glistened in the morning sun along the banks of the Connecticut River. It had been a year since David left Durham to go back to Haddam. He was living with the Rev. Phineas Fiske, who was in his twenty-third year of ministry there and the second pastor of the town. Although David still battled over whether or not he really believed Jesus Christ to be his Lord and Savior, he wanted to become a minister of the gospel anyway; and maybe even a missionary to the Indians. But now, more than ever, he wanted to pursue his studies and even attend college.

Pastor Fiske died in the fall of 1739 and David went to live with his brother, Nehemiah. Nehemiah had married one of Fiske's six daughters, Elizabeth, and was also a minister in Haddam. He had gone to Yale and was quickly becoming the example for David.

Although David didn't mind living with Nehemiah, he often felt lonely and homeless. Wanting direction and purpose, he took a walk on the unusually cool evening of July 12th, 1739. He eventually found himself wandering about in a secluded hazel grove east of town, when something extraordinary happened.

He went there to pray, but felt uneasy and discouraged about his own spiritual condition and hard heart toward God. He struggled in prayer to God for over half an hour when, suddenly, God shattered his stony heart and gave him a new heart—a heart that loved Jesus Christ! He was saved from his sins and from eternal hell by God's amazing grace because he knew, like all mankind, he didn't deserve to be saved!

That evening, David faced heaven and closed his eyes and wept with tears of joy and of freedom. "I love you, my God," he exclaimed. "I am so pleased and satisfied that you alone are God over all; that you alone are eternal and unchanging!"

David was wholly pleased with God's perfections and character and his heart was overflowing with delight in God. Though he had wrestled with God's sovereign will in saving people before, he then knew that his salvation was based solely on God's grace. He knew that the foundation of his salvation rested upon Christ's perfect righteousness and his death on the cross for his sins.

David continued to pray in the grove for a while, recounting the wonder of God's creation and how he is in complete control of everything that happens. He knew now that God was calling him into ministry. But, like all ministers of that day, he needed to prepare for ministry by going to school.

Two months later, in September 1739, Brainerd entered Yale College in New Haven, Connecticut.

* * *

"Hey, Brainerd. Go and grab some more rolls for me," yelled a short eighteen-year-old boy named Peter, who happened to be an upper classman at Yale during David's freshman year.

David didn't say anything, but quietly got up from his seat and walked over to the serving table, where he asked for some rolls. All of the sudden, a soft but firm object hit him in the back of the head and he ducked down (as if to dodge another flying roll), only to see a half-eaten piece of bread lying on the floor at his feet. He looked up and saw a row of upper classmen all laughing. What made matters worse was that they were all younger than David. As a twenty-one-year-old freshman, he was older than most of the upper classmen, which made his position all the more embarrassing.

He brought the rolls back over to Peter and offered the plate. Peter looked up, took the rolls, and frowned at David. "You can go sit down now," he said with a slight chuckle, nudging the guy next to him.

The constant ridicule and hazing—being forced to do menial tasks for the upper classmen—was directed not only at David, but at all of the incoming freshmen. It was part and parcel of life at College Hall at Yale. It didn't bother him personally, but rather he found their conduct—indeed, many of the students' conduct—quite out of step with the Christian life. And what made matters worse was that many of the students at Yale were preparing for ministry!

After dinner, David walked up to his dormitory where he slept, which was a skinny three-story building with little privacy. He lit the lanterns that lined the hallway leading to his room, the wood floor creaking beneath his feet. In his room were two small desks, two cushioned cots and two bookshelves—one for him and one for his roommate.

After lighting a few candles around the room, he walked over to the single window and felt the cool October air seeping in around the frame. He was alone. Some of the other young men were studying together near the campus library and others had planned a night of frolic and "fun".

He walked back toward his desk, sat down, and opened his theology textbook, which covered the basics of the nature of God, the sinfulness of man, salvation through Jesus Christ, the doctrine of the Bible, and an understanding of the end times. But just as he flipped through to find his evening assignment, he heard a loud yell outside his window. Jumping up, David ran back to the window and tried to peer out into the twilight evening—finally finding a group of his classmates running past the end of the building. Towards the front of the building he saw one of his professors yelling at them.

It was not uncommon for some of the guys to get drunk, play cards, and even steal or break windows around New Haven. "How could these men, preparing for the Lord's service, do such things?" David wondered still peering past the end of the building. He closed his eyes and rested his head against the window. "Am I really any better because I do not do those sins?"

A rush of guilt and shame flooded his head and he felt his heart pound in his chest. "I am so wretched and vile!" he whispered. "I hate my sin and I want to feel forgiven and clean!"

He walked over, sat back down at his desk and buried his face in his hands, praying to God and wrestling over his sin.

"Heavenly Father, I do not feel any comfort from your love tonight. I cannot find your mercy right now! Please grant me greater faith. I want to rest in your grace!"

He spent the rest of that evening, like many other evenings, in anguish and feeling little hope or delight in his thoughts on God. Unfortunately, this was a regular pattern for David – a burden he would carry throughout his life.

* * *

Over the next few months, David took great joy in his studies and excelled beyond most of the other students. He loved the challenge so much, however, that his academic pursuits suppressed his spiritual life even more. He spent less and less time in fellowship with God and reading his Word. But God, in his infinite wisdom, often grabs our attention through affliction.

David suddenly woke up in a cold sweat feeling completely disoriented and dazed. He sat up and glanced around the dark room. The moonlight cast a faint glow over the few pieces of furniture.

He felt his forehead with his hand and quickly realized that he had a high fever. The room was cold, but he was completely soaked with sweat. He knew he needed to leave immediately to go back home to his family to recover.

A measles epidemic had broken out at the college the week prior and David had hoped to avoid it. Many of the other students had already left, but David was committed to getting ahead in his studies. Getting sick back then was very dangerous and often resulted in death and David knew he needed help.

The next day, some friends rode with him back to Haddam. It was a blessing in disguise, for David had resolved to slow down with his studies and enjoy sweeter communion with his Savior through prayer and meditation.

When he got back to school a couple of weeks later, he made a regular practice of going into the woods alone to be with God and delighted in God's glorious character and grace. That spring and summer brought him greater opportunity to find strength in the gospel and fellowship with his Lord. Though he was a great sinner, he had a greater Savior. His sins had been completely forgiven and now God looked upon David as if he was looking upon his own Son. David was adopted into God's family through the merits of Jesus!

It seemed as if life was going well ... almost too well.

Expelled!
July 1740

The bitter wine burned David's throat and he thought about his sin and Christ's bitter death on the cross. He walked back to his seat in the chapel and bowed his head in prayer.

"Jesus, as I ponder the crown of thorns thrust onto your head, I know you deserved a crown of gold – a crown fit for a King! The lashings across your back, the beatings by soldiers, the ridicule, and the nails through your hands and feet – all to pay for my sin! I am so unworthy! I am so–"

"Why don't you just drink it all!" whispered a fellow student behind him to the other men on his row.

David stopped in his prayer and listened to the row of guys behind him all laughing under their breath. He couldn't believe what he was hearing.

"I will drink it all later this evening," the young man responded with a slightly louder laugh. "Are you going to the pub, John?"

"Of course! But I must write that laborious essay on the doctrine of Christ first – what a waste of my time!"

David couldn't take it any longer. He turned around and snapped: "Are you so disrespectful to be talking like this, especially as we feast on Christ spiritually in his Supper?" The younger men all looked shocked and immediately looked down at their feet.

"Shame on you!"

David turned back around and bowed his head; he was angry. He couldn't understand how people who professed their love for Jesus could, at the same time, not talk about it or show it in how they lived. It was almost as if they had no sensitivity to their calling as future ministers of the gospel!

After Communion, David walked back toward his dormitory, feeling slight relief and excitement in the approaching fall semester of study. He desired to learn as much as he could about the excellencies of Christ and about God's Word.

As he walked, he noticed the burning in his throat didn't go away. In fact, he felt like his throat was on fire. He stopped and put his hand over his mouth – coughing to clear the mucus. When he removed his hand, it was covered in blood!

"I'm coughing up blood!" he whispered to himself in shock.

Suddenly, David felt a cold chill shoot down his spine and the reality of what was happening set in. He spit the remaining blood out of his mouth and coughed again into his hand – just to make sure. Again, blood! The fleeting delight in his future study quickly started to flee all the more.

David contracted tuberculosis, a bacterial disease that attacks the lungs and other organs of the body and usually was very deadly. He knew of many who had died from the disease and its effects were well known.

Over the next week, he began to feel worse. He was exhausted, confined to his bed from fevers and loss of appetite. As he began to lose weight, his fellow classmates knew he didn't have the strength to continue with school. They brought him to Haddam once again with sickness to rest and recover.

Three months later, he was well enough to return to college. Although many times he longed to be with God in heaven and depart from this life of suffering and misery, he knew it wasn't his time yet.

But when David returned to Yale, something extraordinary was happening!

* * *

The cold November air blew through the leafless trees as David made his way to New Haven once again to continue his education. Even the sound of rustling leaves and the rhythmic trot of his horse couldn't steer his mind away from the classes, the books, and his classmates that awaited him. More than ever, he was resolved to learn and to grow in the Lord.

Instead of going to the college itself, he rode to the home of Isaac Dickerman, who was deputy to the General Assembly and captain of the militia in 1722. Dickerman had a son who had died earlier that year and left a vacant room in his house for young Brainerd to live while in school. The lack of spiritual interest among his fellow classmates annoyed David and so he acquired permission to live off campus in Dickerman's home.

As David approached Dickerman's home, he saw a large man standing in front of the door, as if he were expecting David.

"Well, well, young Brainerd – how are you feeling?" called the middle-aged man in a rather gruff voice; the kind of voice you get after yelling for years of your life.

Brainerd jumped off his horse. "Quite well, sir."

"Good, good."

Brainerd walked up the steps and shook hands with his new landlord. "I am most grateful that you have opened your home for me to live. And …" David paused, not knowing how to go on. "I am deeply sorry for the loss of your son, Mr. Dickerman."

"Thank you, David." The man looked down as if inspecting his boots. "It has been difficult, but God has called my son into his eternal rest where we shall meet again."

"Indeed," Brainerd said with a slight nod of his head.

Dickerman took the satchel from David's hand. "Well, come on in. I have a warm fire and some tea inside and I want to hear all about your plans AND …" He stopped and smiled at David. "I have some news for you that you might find most pleasant."

That evening, after David got settled into his new room, he and Mr. Dickerman sat down together and talked about all the many things that had happened while David was gone.

"The Rev. George Whitefield, whom you no doubt know about, came and preached just a week or two ago – it was October 27th – to all the students." Dickerman leaned forward in his rocking chair and peered at David. "He preached with such boldness and sincerity! The Holy Spirit fell upon the students mightily and many have not ceased in prayer and repentance and confession – the whole town, it seems, has been taken by a conviction of sin and a renewed zeal for the things of God!"

David was in shock. "You mean to say, that my classmates have had a revival?"

"Yes! Tomorrow, you shall see." He paused, sat back in his chair and took a sip of tea. "The local ministers have been serving double time with students coming to them for spiritual guidance and exhortation from God's Word."

This was certainly a wonderful surprise for Brainerd. Indeed, he had heard of Whitefield and the marvelous preaching he had done in Northampton in Jonathan Edwards' pulpit, a month earlier.

A revival had been spreading all over New England from the preaching of George Whitefield, who was becoming famous for his powerful sermons and his amazingly loud voice – able to speak to thousands at one time.

Whitefield was born in 1714 in Gloucester, England. He was converted while attending Oxford University and was ordained to gospel ministry in the Anglican church by the Bishop of Gloucester. Because the Church of England had not assigned him a pulpit, he began preaching in the open air, which was a relatively new practice. Immediately, crowds, at times numbering in the thousands, began to flock to hear him.

When he arrived in America in 1740, he began preaching to crowds nearly every day. This continued for months and the Spirit of God began converting people by the thousands as he traveled throughout the colonies. Whitefield was a Calvinist who preached that salvation was the work of God alone, but he always freely offered the gospel to all who heard.

Crossing the Atlantic Ocean some thirteen times, preaching over an estimated 18,000 formal sermons, and winning the support of both the poor and the rich (like Benjamin Franklin), George Whitefield quickly became one of the most popular preachers of all time.

Rumors spread across New Haven and the Yale campus before Whitefield arrived and his delivery of Scripture matched the anticipation. A revival had started and David Brainerd was thrilled to be in the company of so many who loved Christ as their greatest treasure!

Early in December, he ventured out into the cold morning to walk and talk with God. As he reflected on the book of Hebrews in the Bible, he lifted up his voice: "Oh! One hour with God infinitely exceeds all the pleasures and delights of this lower world."

The flames of revival were fanned further through the preaching of a thirty-eight year old Presbyterian pastor from New Jersey, Gilbert Tennent. Tennent preached seventeen times in New Haven over a course of a week and many of the students were taken up in a frenzy over his preaching – and even followed him thirty miles to the town of Milford the following week.

But not everybody was happy with Whitefield and Tennent, including Thomas Clap, Yale's rector. Clap believed that the so-called "revival" was nothing more than a stirring of emotions, with no real and lasting change in the students. He strictly forbade the students from going to Milford to hear Tennent preach. When the students disobeyed Clap's warning, he fined them.

Despite Clap's skepticism, the revival continued and Brainerd began visiting fellow classmates and others around New Haven, inquiring about the condition of their souls. Many were saved during Brainerd's visits, including Samuel Hopkins, who went on to become one of New England's greatest theologians.

The Great Awakening, as the revival became known as, established over 100 churches to the already existing 400 churches in New England.

Suddenly there was a shortage of trained ministers of the gospel and people began "preaching" without license and without training.

Some, who encouraged the new churches and were taken up by the revivals, became known as the "New Side." Others, who valued the old ways of preaching and historic faith, became known as the "Old Side."

Tensions between the "New Side" and the "Old Side" came to a head in September 1741 when a man named James Davenport came and preached in New Haven. During his sermon, he implied the lack of spirituality among some of the local ministers and made negative statements about Yale's rector – Thomas Clap – as well as its trustees and tutors. As a result, the trustees of Yale met that month and passed this resolution:

"Voted, that if any student of this college shall directly or indirectly say, that the Rector, either of the trustees or tutors are hypocrites, carnal or unconverted men, he shall for the first offense make a public confession in the Hall, and for the second offense be expelled."

* * *

"That was one long prayer meeting, wouldn't you say, David?"

David looked around the College Hall and watched the remaining students leave through the back door. "Indeed, it was. Sometimes I think that Whittelsey—" he paused and looked around the room again.

"Whittelsey what?"

David looked back at his two friends who had stayed with him. "I'd rather not say."

"David, we just want to know what you think of him. You know he is strongly opposed to this Awakening. In fact, he—"

"I know. You could tell in his prayers tonight," David said, finding a dark wooden chair nearby to sit in.

Chauncey Whittelsey was one of Yale's finest tutors and came from a well-known family who opposed the revivals that were happening across Connecticut. Besides his knowledge of Hebrew, Greek, and Latin, he was also well learned in the liberal arts and sciences. A gifted individual, Chauncey was only six months older than Brainerd and had started teaching at Yale at the same time David arrived.

His two friends kept insisting that he tell them his thoughts of Whittelsey. "What do you think of his spiritual condition, David?" one of them asked.

David looked at the worn wooden arm rests of his chair and rubbed the end of the arm rest with his hand as if he was trying to get a smudge off. "Whittelsey has no more grace than this chair!"

One of his friends leaned over and patted him on the shoulder. "Well, there we have it!"

All of a sudden, they heard something that sounded like feet running away down the outside of the main hall and out the door closest to their dormitory. The three friends looked at each other, hoping that their conversation wasn't about to be reported.

The next morning, while Brainerd was studying at his desk, a loud knock broke the silence and made him jump. The door opened and in walked a young freshman with a scowl on his face.

"You are requested to go see Rector Clap immediately, Mr. Brainerd."

David slowly stood up and closed his book on his desk. "Do you know what occasion elicits this meeting?"

The young freshman looked petrified and began to blush. "You need to go now, sir."

As David made his way out of his dorm and toward Clap's office, he couldn't help but think of the comment he made the night before about Whittelsey. "That comment was made in private," he thought to himself. "What is said in private is for private audiences only—I cannot be at fault for that."

As he walked on, he began thinking of other things he might have done and thought about his recent visit to a forbidden prayer meeting a couple of weeks prior. David had gone to a worship service that Clap had strictly forbidden the students attending for fear that such a service would draw his students away from the "Old Side" view of the historic faith and would promote a rising, negative view of the Yale faculty.

"Surely attending that meeting is not a serious offense," he kept thinking to himself as he walked.

When David arrived at Clap's office, he knocked on the door.

"Come in," gruffed a deep and seemingly frustrated voice.

David opened the door and walked in, his hands shaking a bit.

Clap motioned that David sit down. "Mr. Brainerd, I have been informed of something terribly disappointing from one of your fellow classmates."

A confused look spread across David's face.

"I have been told that last night, you said that our tutor, Chauncey Whittelsey, had no more grace than a chair."

Clap peered at him. "Is this true, Mr. Brainerd?"

David knew about the resolution that the trustees had passed only a few weeks prior and thoughts of the consequences began bubbling up in his head.

"Is this true?" Clap repeated, though with more resolve and sternness.

David glanced at his boots. "Yes, sir. But it was a private conversation and was not meant to be—"

"That does not change the fact that you have greatly insulted one of our own tutors!" Clap barked back, standing up from behind his desk. "You shall make a public apology and confession of this incident tonight. I will inform the student body—this will not be tolerated on this campus!"

David felt his throat burning, but didn't want to clear it for fear that blood would come up again.

"What say you, Mr. Brainerd?"

His voice shaky, both from fear and from his burning throat, he managed a feeble response: "I shall not make a public confession and apology for my actions because they were said in private and were injuriously pulled out from me by my friends."

By this point, Clap's face was flush red. "You will make such an apology or you shall be expelled from this school, Mr. Brainerd. You dare not test me on this."

"I will not and that is final, Rector Clap. I feel that I have been wronged in this matter and—"

"Please leave, Mr. Brainerd!"

David slowly stood up, put on his cap and walked out of his office.

* * *

That evening, after David had eaten dinner, he retired to his room to study and pray. But when he arrived at his room, he noticed a piece of paper that was partially sticking out from beneath his door. Opening the door, he picked it up and opened it. It read:

Whereas Mr. David Brainerd, sophomore student at Yale College, has violated official resolution of this institution and, whereas he remains unwilling to confess such sin and apologize publically before the Yale student assembly, the officials of this College do hereby expel Mr. Brainerd from Yale, effective immediately.

David couldn't believe what he was reading. He had been expelled! He walked over to his chair and took off his scarf, throwing it on his bed.

"How could this have happened, all so suddenly?" he thought to himself as he sat down. "How can I be a minister of the Gospel of Jesus Christ and not have education? No church will call me to be their pastor with no formal education."

He crinkled up the piece of paper in his hand and threw it on the ground. He was angry—at himself and at the school administration. Part of him felt that he was wronged and another part felt that he was the one who was wrong.

The cold winter air only added to his chilled soul. He felt dead to God and had no desire for ministry. Where would he go? What was he to do now? Would David have no impact on the history of the world? Would his chances of making a difference be over? Perhaps. But God has made foolish the wisdom of man and in his mysterious providence, believers can find rest for their troubled souls.

A Call in the Woods
1742

The thick morning fog made seeing nearly impossible. In the distance, David could hear a faint call of some sort of bird, though it did nothing to break the quietness of the morning. It was early, but the sun was already beginning to illuminate the dense cloud— making the entire forest spring to life in a warm orange and red hue.

David sat down on a mossy rock with his back against a large oak tree and looked straight up the trunk of the tree. Small bright-green buds covered the branches above and the deadness of the winter was losing its bite. The signs of early spring gave him an excitement for the warmer months ahead—the fishing, swimming, and not having the constant duties of maintaining a fire throughout the day.

As he continued to look up, thoughts of school flooded his mind and he felt, at once, a deep sense of regret and remorse over saying what he did about that tutor and his actions that followed with Rector Clap. Part of him still felt that he was wronged, but he knew his attitude wasn't pure either.

He looked back down at the rock on which he sat and felt the cold, damp moss with his fingers. He immediately felt inclined to fellowship with God in prayer:

"Heavenly Father, thou art King of Heaven and Earth and there is none like thee. Why hast thou chosen me, a vile and poor sinner, to serve in thy church? I repent of my awful arrogance and pride and petition that thou will cast them away from me and restore to me the joy of my salvation! O, Lord, I offer my heart to thee for correction and change."

All of a sudden, he heard breaking twigs behind him and he poked his head around the tree to spot a young deer eating from some of the low-lying bushes nearby. "Food!" flashed through his mind like a blazing lantern. But he had set apart this day for fasting and prayer.

Fasting usually went along with prayer for David. The constant pains of being hungry were to remind him that Jesus was his true bread of life. They were to remind him of his daily need for Christ and they focused his attention on spending time with the Lord throughout the day—every time he felt hungry. In fact, Jesus said it would be a normal pattern for his followers.

As David looked at the young deer eating, he again turned his attention to God in prayer:

"Lord God, unlike this deer, this world is not my home. I am a pilgrim, passing through toward my true home in heaven with you. Help me love this world less and less and long for the world to come more and more. Oh, Lord, may I never loiter on my heavenly journey!"

Over the course of the next few hours, he wrestled with God in prayer over his sin, over God's grace and glories of the gospel—like Jacob wrestling with the angel until he was blessed. David prayed so fervently, pouring out his soul to God, that he came to realize he was soaked with sweat, even though the morning was quite cold!

After David was expelled from Yale, he had moved to the town of Ripton, about ten miles west of New Haven, to live with a man named Jedediah Mills. Mills was the pastor at Ripton and a Yale graduate. By 1742, Mills had fallen into disfavor with some of the Yale officials because of his strong evangelistic preaching and friendship with some people on the "New Side."

The "Old Side," "New Side" split was still very deep across New England. The Old Side held to orthodox teaching and strong education, and were generally against the Christian revivals that were sweeping through the land. They felt that the revivals were nothing but show and that they were "forcing" the Holy Spirit to convert sinners, which was against their theology.

The New Side, on the other hand, embraced the new excitement over God and his Word. They supported preachers who may not have had formal religious education and training. As they saw it, God was using them to bring scores of men and women to trust in Jesus as their Lord and Savior for the first time.

They often believed that the Old Side represented a cold, dead religion that needed new life and vitality.

David tended to lean toward the New Side because he favored what God was doing in convicting sinners and bringing the lost into his church. He also was a victim of the Old Side establishment while at Yale—expelled for casting judgment on one of its tutors.

Ripton provided Brainerd with a welcoming home and a place where he could study religion and prepare for gospel ministry. Pastor Mills readily accepted Brainerd into his home and, during the spring of 1742, taught him theology and the practice of pastoral ministry. Though it wasn't Yale, it was sufficient for young Brainerd.

More than anything else, however, David enjoyed frequent time alone with God in the woods surrounding Ripton. Carving out substantial time during the day to commune with God through prayer was very important for him. Many mornings, he would retreat early into the nearby forest to pray and to meditate on the Bible.

Bible meditation had only been a part of the church for less than two hundred years. It wasn't until the Protestant Reformation in the early-to-mid 1500s that the laity—the church members—read and studied the Bible on their own. Before then, the Bible of the church was only in Latin, which most people couldn't read. But the Protestant Reformation released the Bible into the hands of the people and their joy and delight in God grew, causing a revival and reformation across Europe.

Later, Reformers in England, known as Puritans, eventually carried the importance of Bible reading and meditation to the shores of the New World, America. Though some thought of the Puritans as cold, humorless Christians, they had an incredible joy in God and wanted to pursue Jesus with all of their heart, soul, mind, and strength.

Bible meditation, for Brainerd, meant taking a small portion of Scripture and reading it over and over again—praying frequently over its content that God would apply the truths found therein to his own mind, heart, and soul. It meant thinking about a word or phrase until he felt blessed by it or utterly convicted of his own sin. Meditating on the Bible became a regular practice for David and a source of extreme delight and satisfaction in God.

Throughout the course of that spring, David's knowledge of and love for God grew, but so did his sense of God's calling on his life. He felt that God was still calling him into ministry, even though he had been expelled from college. For most people, being expelled would have dashed all hopes of entering the ministry to pieces. But not for David. God's calling on his life ran deeper than formal education.

His preparation for ministry finally came to a head on July 29th, 1742.

* * *

"What is the chief end of man?" asked the rather large-framed man with an array of open books on the table before him.

David stood before them and was starting to feel less and less confident about his answers: "Let me think for a moment," he said pausing to scratch his head. It was an answer he'd known even as a child. Surely he could remember it. Thankfully he did! "To glorify God and to enjoy him forever. That is the answer to question number one of the Westminster Shorter Catechism, sir."

"Very good, Mr. Brainerd. Next."

The hot July sun was beaming through the large windows looking over the western hills and David could feel beads of sweat beginning to run down his face. This exam was unlike any other he had taken—standing before a row of men, each with their books and Bibles open, shooting question after question at the quivering examinee.

"Name the three major covenants that frame our understanding of covenant theology."

David was fairly familiar with the biblical covenants—the covenant with Adam, Noah, Abraham, Moses, David, and, of course, the New Covenant established by Christ himself in the upper room before his betrayal. But the major covenants—he had to think about this one.

"The Covenant of Life, also called the Covenant of Works—"

"Yes, go on," gruffed the gentleman impatiently.

"The Covenant of Grace and … the Covenant of Redemption."

"Very good, David. What is the Covenant of Redemption and where would you find such a doctrine in the Bible?"

David's mind raced through the pages of Scripture as if fumbling through a file cabinet looking for a lost document. "In John, chapter 17, we find the prayer of our Lord Jesus, where he said that he has not lost one whom the Father had given him. In other words, Jesus fulfilled his end of an agreement—a covenant—established before the foundation of the world between him and the Father."

The older man sat back in his chair. "Well said, young lad. Well said."

For the next three hours, David fielded questions regarding theology, knowledge of the Bible and how to craft a sermon from the Old and New Testaments. It was similar to any other licensure exam of that day, except for one key factor. The exam was given by a newly formed New Side group called *The Association of the Eastern District of Fairfield County*—an association not recognized as "official" by the Old Side ministers around the New Haven area.

Several New Side ministers had become dissatisfied with the anti-revival leanings of many of the older established ministers and felt that they were squelching the Holy Spirit. So in the summer of 1742, they formed their own ecclesiastical body to examine and license ministerial candidates, like David Brainerd.

"Mr Brainerd, we have one final question for you. How would you preach Christ Jesus from, say, the book of Joshua in the Old Testament?"

David took a moment to reflect on the key themes of Joshua and remembered the book being about the new leader of Israel leading the people into the Promised Land. He looked up and spoke with conviction and passion:

"As Joshua led God's people out of the desert into the land God had promised them, so Christ, our Lord, leads us out of sin and death into the new Promised Land, the new Jerusalem and our eternal home—heaven. And—"

"Yes, go on."

"And as Joshua led God's people in battle, defeating the enemies of God, so Christ Jesus has fought and defeated our great foe—Satan himself—and, therefore, has defeated death forever on our behalf!"

After the exam was over, as the examination committee deliberated, David took a deep breath and waited for the results.

"Mr David Brainerd—"

David stood up straight as if about to hear a charge.

"By the powers of this association of ministers and under the authority of Christ as King, we hereby license you to preach the gospel of Jesus Christ. Well done, sir, and God bless."

He passed! He was thrilled and could not wait to step into a pulpit and deliver a sermon.

"Thank you all and God's peace be with you!" David said with a big smile.

Though he was now licensed, he was not yet ordained, which meant that he was not yet allowed to administer the sacraments of baptism and the Lord's Supper.

The next day, David traveled to Southbury to preach his very first sermon at John Graham's church. It would be an event he would never forget.

* * *

Even though it was a Friday, the people kept filing into the church building to hear the new, young preacher. After several minutes, the talking ceased and all eyes fixated on Brainerd as he ascended into the pulpit.

"Lord, may your holy Word go forth and not return void," David prayed to himself as he looked over the anxious crowd.

"Please hear the Word of God from 1 Peter 4:8. 'And above all things have fervent charity among yourselves: for charity shall cover a multitude of sins'."

David felt a divine presence like never before and was encouraged by the Spirit using him as he began to proclaim the good news of Jesus.

"Charity is a fruit of Christian humility and the opposite of selfish ambition. Notice that the Apostle Peter does not say that we are to simply have charity, but fervent charity. This characteristic should be a distinguishing mark in your life together."

As he continued, the glorious display of Jesus came out in bright array.

"Believer in Christ: why should you extend such charity to one another? It is surely because of the charity, the love and the grace extended to us by the eternal Ancient of Days taking on flesh as the Infant of Days. We have the power to display charity toward each other because charity has been displayed first and foremost in the gospel of Jesus Christ. Love, then, for you were first loved by God!"

The people of that little church in Southbury came under the power and conviction of the Holy Spirit in a mighty way and Brainerd had stepped into his God-given calling—a calling embraced humbly and with a whole heart.

Nine days later, Brainerd stepped into the pulpit of the Reverend Joseph Bellamy's church in Bethlehem, Connecticut to preach on Job 14:14: "If a man die, shall he live again?" Again, the Holy Spirit illumined the hearts of his hearers that morning and Brainerd experienced the fruit of his preaching once more.

Bellamy was a gifted man, graduating from Yale at age sixteen, studying under Jonathan Edwards for two years, and then called to be Bethlehem's first pastor at age eighteen. He would go on to serve that congregation for over fifty years!

Brainerd and Bellamy shared a similar vision of ministry—both being New Side ministers who loved to see the lost coming to know Jesus as Lord and Savior. The Thursday following David's sermon, their partnership in ministry took them on a new adventure that would characterize the rest of David's short life—sharing the gospel with Indians!

The Traveling Preacher
August 1742

They rode fast through the forest in the cool of the morning, their horses' manes wet with sweat. They wanted to reach the Scaticock Indians early enough to spend the whole day preaching and teaching them about the only hope in this earthly life—Jesus Christ—and make it back to Bethlehem by nightfall.

While they were riding, David suddenly felt a deep and overwhelming sense of his own unworthiness. "Why would God choose me to do this—the chief of sinners?" he thought to himself. "I feel that I am worse than any devil! Why would you let me live another minute?" David looked back at Bellamy, whose face seemed so confident and resolved with gospel purpose. He looked on ahead again. "These natives do not want to hear me preach—what am I doing?"

As they approached the Scaticock village and saw bands of Indians cooking over fires and sharpening pieces of rock, these thoughts evolved into a stomach pain of being in the wrong place at the wrong time! They weren't totally sure that these Indians would be friendly and welcome them. At any moment, their lives could be over. They could be taken prisoner or worse—be offered up as a burnt offering to the "spirit gods" of their religion. They were utterly at the will of a remote tribe of Indians who, as a whole, were slowly being pushed more and more into the American west.

To David's surprise, as they trotted into the heart of the village, the children came in swarms with smiles and open arms. He was shocked! These Indians had had business and even religious dealings with the "white man" before, but stories and rumors of Indians attacking on the frontier often sent fear into an initial meeting … like this one. Some of the Indians even knew a little English and could translate into their local language. In fact, translation work with various Indian tribes had become a vital part of business relationships, peace initiatives and, of course, missionary labors.

"Greetings!" called out Bellamy to the crowd of people who had all seemed to stop whatever it was they were doing and were slowly walking toward the two men. "We have come in the name of our Lord and Savior Jesus Christ and would desire that you hear our message of hope and peace this day."

They heard one of the Indians talking rather loudly to the others and assumed he was a translator.

"Do you speak English?" Bellamy asked, pointing to the middle-aged man who was holding a large spear upright next to him.

The man immediately stood straight up. "Yes, I do."

"Very well. Would you mind translating for us today?"

Wanting to get some practice conversing in English, the native had no hesitancy about his answer. "Yes, yes, that will be good!"

After dismounting and creating somewhat of a make shift platform from a stack of wood, David stepped up and started to preach from Job 14:14: "If a man die, shall he live again?" It was the same verse he had preached on the day before at Bellamy's church. He went on to talk about the grace of God in the gospel of Jesus Christ, who said, "I am the resurrection and the life. Whoever believes in me, though he die, yet shall he live" (John 11:25).

The Holy Spirit empowered David to preach and attended his preaching so that the Indians even cried out for mercy and were greatly distressed over their spiritual state apart from a relationship with Jesus. Though David's day began with intense attack from Satan and an overwhelming sense of unworthiness, God used David to speak to these Indians in a mighty way.

David and Joseph Bellamy traveled back to Bethlehem that evening where David preached several more times at Bellamy's church before heading to New Haven. That is right: New Haven! The thought of going back to New Haven brought about a flurry of dreadful feelings because of his expulsion from Yale and the many people who didn't like him there. But he went anyway and stayed for the remainder of August—preaching to and praying with people just about every day.

But while he was in there, certain individuals plotted to trap him and have him arrested for preaching without an "official" license. The Connecticut General Assembly had passed legislation the previous May that prohibited itinerant evangelists (like Brainerd) from preaching town to town. They felt that these evangelists were stirring up trouble and fanning the flame of the "Old Side", "New Side" controversies that were widespread across New England.

Certain people in New Haven, therefore, felt that David had violated the law by coming to New Haven and preaching. But before their plans came to fruition, David escaped to the nearby town of Judea. He now knew that he wasn't welcome there and thought it such an irony that, while the natives who didn't know Christ accepted him and welcomed him, his own fellow Christians wanted to have him imprisoned!

* * *

On October 23rd, 1742, David set out on a 175-mile preaching journey on horseback. More than ever, inner conflicts and battles over his own sin and unworthiness for the calling to which God had called him raged in his mind and heart. He felt that he was under constant spiritual attack, which made sense because he was preaching against Satan's schemes and pointing people toward the Savior of sinners. Satan doesn't want God's plan to go forward and does everything he can to hinder the advancement of the gospel of Christ.

Despite these inner conflicts, he disciplined himself to spend time in prayer alone in the woods and to meditate on God's Word. Both of these disciplines greatly encouraged his soul and revived his heart when he was battling feelings of sadness, anxiety and depression.

Over the next few months, David's preaching ministry from town to town took him over 1,200 miles, preaching over sixty sermons to countless men and women. He wanted to wear himself out in service to the Lord and when he felt weak and tired, he was reminded of what Christ Jesus said to Paul in 2 Corinthians 12:9: "My grace is sufficient for you, for my power is made perfect in weakness." His love to see the lost come and know the saving knowledge that Jesus lived a life we should have lived and died a death we should have died, was his singular driving passion.

Toward the end of this preaching stint, he was traveling to New Haven to stay with some friends—outside of town this time—when he got word that his older brother, Nehemiah, was ill with tuberculosis. David looked up to his brother who was now thirty years old. He had been a role model and example for David for all of his life, but on 9th November, Nehemiah passed from this life to the next. David took it hard, but knew that we all are mere pilgrims in this short earthly life, just passing through to our true heavenly home. In fact, he had prayed for his younger brother (who had just started at Yale that autumn semester) that he would become more and more of a stranger in his earthly journey. The Brainerds were ready to die; the Indians weren't. They needed to hear the gospel message and David knew that God was calling him to that end!

* * *

One of the primary goals of early settlers in the New England colonies was to evangelize the native Indians. Though many had fled England from religious persecution to the new land, stories and rumors stirred their hopes of seeing the lost natives of America come to know Jesus as Savior and Lord.

Many early New England ministers witnessed many Indians become Christians, but the missionary cause was dealt a devastating blow during the years of 1675-6 in one of the bloodiest wars on American soil: King Philip's War. Indian chief, Metacomet, known to the English as "King Philip," became increasingly angry over colonials infringing on Wampanoag lands and led a series of attacks on the English settlers, resulting in an all-out war between the colonials and the natives.

Of the ninety towns in New England during those years, over half were attacked—many on both sides killed and many homes burned to the ground. While some Indian tribes pitched in to help the English settlers—for they were enemies of the Wampanoag tribe even before the English arrived—the conflict brought greater tension between the settlers and the natives. The war crippled the spiritual work of the early missionaries and now added a stronger barrier for future evangelism.

Twenty five years later, a group of men in Scotland wanted to help further the gospel through evangelism in different areas of the world and organized the Society in Scotland for Propagating Christian Knowledge. Later known as the "Scottish Society," this organization initially carried out ministry and evangelism in the Highlands of Scotland amongst both Roman Catholics and the ignorant. But by 1730, it set its sight on New England—doing missions among the Indians. For ten years, the numbers of Indians converted varied, but they were resolved to keep going.

In 1740, the Scottish Society set up a New York Board to oversee missionaries and their work in the Middle Colonies and two years later, toward the end of 1742, that Board contacted David Brainerd! The letter informed him that the Scottish Society wanted Brainerd to travel to New York to meet with the Board concerning a possible missionary employment.

David was thrilled! This was the chance that he had been praying for. At once, however, he was seized with an overwhelming burden of responsibility and weight of what this would mean for him. After praying with a few friends in New Haven and in Ripton, he rode for three days, traveling nearly eighty-five miles to New York. As he was entering into the city, he was at once overcome with confusion and noise. He immediately whipped out his journal to write:

"Wednesday, November 24th. Came to New York; still felt concerned about the importance of my business; put up many earnest requests to God for his help and direction; was confused with the noise and tumult of the city; enjoyed but little time alone with God; but my soul longed after him."

Indeed, the experience was overwhelming to David. The next day, he was examined in the areas of theology, biblical knowledge and even his preaching—not to be licensed to preach—but to serve as one of the Scottish Society's missionaries to the Indians.

* * *

Ebenezer Pemberton kept drilling David over and over on particular areas of theology and what David might do in various pastoral and evangelistic situations.

"Tell me, Mr. Brainerd, what qualified you for ministry in the first place?"

David looked down in thought. He knew he felt unworthy and so sinfully vile and yet believed that God had called him to do missionary work among the Indians.

"To be honest, Mr. Pemberton," David began, "I know that I am a wretched sinner and that all my heart is tainted with the fall. I also know that I do not deserve such a high calling to be in the missionary service of our Lord. But I have witnessed God use me in preaching his Word and felt the Spirit's presence in such circumstances. I have also enjoyed the encouragement of the church, which has supported me in such endeavors." He paused and stood straight up. "Therefore, Mr. Pemberton, I believe that God, and no man, has qualified me to proclaim the excellencies of Christ, though I am nothing in and of myself."

"Very well, young Brainerd," said Pemberton with a delighted look on his face.

After the exam was finished, and after David preached to a large gathering of souls at Pemberton's church in Wall Street, the Board met to discuss the possibility of David's service among the Indians. They finally finished and brought David in to their meeting room.

"Mr Brainerd, we as the Board of Commissioners of the Scottish Society find you to be a highly suitable candidate for missionary service. We, therefore, appoint you as a missionary to minister to the Indians living near the Forks of the Delaware River and along the Susquehanna River in Pennsylvania. It is our desire that you go as soon as would be convenient for you."

David now had a clear calling, funding from a missionary society and a deep joy and excitement over his future. He couldn't help but think about what it might look like for him on the frontier preaching to scores of lost souls and many coming to know Jesus as their Savior and King!

The next day, after spending some more time discussing the details with several of the commissioners, he headed to his hometown of Haddam. He wanted to see his family and friends and attend to some personal business before commencing on his missionary service.

On December 11th, Brainerd preached in John Graham's church in Southbury, where he met a young man named Nehemiah Greenman. Greenman wanted to pursue a calling into the ministry, but didn't have the necessary money to attend college. Even though David needed the money, he took the remainder of the funds from the estate his father had left him and offered to pay for Greenman's education at Yale. Greenman accepted David's offer and went on to graduate in 1748 and pastor a Presbyterian church in New Jersey from 1753 to 1779.

David preached a few more times in different congregations during the remainder of December, always preaching with sincere earnestness that those days might be his last chance to see them. He told his Southbury friends that he supposed it might be likely he should not meet them again until heaven.

One thing was clear in the 1740s. Life in the wilderness on the frontier of Westward expansion was one of the harshest, most dangerous places. There was constant danger of Indian attack, of literally freezing to death in the brutally cold winters, and a constant lack of food. Moreover, there were no hospitals or doctors nearby to provide medical treatment if necessary. When David said he might not see them again, he knew there was a very good chance that he would lay down his life in such a remote location.

It must be remembered, too, that America was not a separate nation at this point. It was a colony of England and ruled by the English monarch. The protection and peace that many in England enjoyed was not a reality in the New World. Uncertainty and a constant fear of the future was part and parcel of New England life, even if settlers had been there for over a hundred years. Traveling from town to town through thick forest without the convenience of any type of shelter, the threat of wild animals, and disease all added to the danger that existed for people living in more remote areas of New England.

During the remainder of December and January, David visited with friends and preached in various churches because the Scottish Society felt that beginning in the dead of the winter was near impossible for a solitary man in the wilderness. But while the external dangers waited, internal spiritual attack and depression was as intense and real as ever. David daily battled distress, dread, and the torments of sinful guilt—to the point that he could barely eat. Moreover, he kept coughing up blood and feeling physically weak. The winter of 1742-43 was also a winter of the soul.

On February 1st, 1743, David rode to the town of East Hampton, a growing whaling community to work alongside a fellow missionary named Azariah Horton. The town had witnessed something of a spiritual awakening and revival and afforded David an adequate place to test his ministry skills until the long winter came to an end.

East Hampton became his home for over a month, though he traveled frequently to other towns to preach. On one such venture in March, he rode to Newark, where he was encouraged in a time of conversation and prayer with Aaron Burr, another Scottish Society correspondent. Burr was a brilliant and devout Christian who later married Jonathan Edwards' daughter, Esther. Their son, Aaron Burr, Jr, went on to become the third Vice President of the United States.

Then on March 21st, David met with the Scottish Society Commissioners at Woodbridge, several miles south of Elizabethtown. A dispute between settlers and Indians at the Forks of the Delaware had escalated into a dangerous situation and such a conflict made the location an extremely difficult place for a missionary, like David, to be accepted. At the same time, the Board had been informed that, through a missionary to the Stockbridge Indians—John Sergeant—God was bringing several Indians to know Jesus and spiritual fruit was seen in the native community of Kaunaumeek, New York, which was located about twenty miles northeast of David's ministry base in Massachusetts.

The Board informed David of his new mission, at least for the time being—evangelism among the Indians at Kaunaumeek. Moreover, he was to study the Algonquian language under the instruction of

Sergeant at Stockbridge. On March 31st, 1743, David arrived at his new mission with mixed feelings of fear and excitement. Would the Indians at Kaunaumeek receive his message of hope and salvation? Would they reject him and chase him out of town? Would they be skeptical of his intentions and seize him or worse— kill him? David didn't know the future, but God did. And he trusted in God's plan for him and prayed that he might not be ashamed, but would have sufficient courage so that Christ would be exalted in his body, whether by life or by death!

A Hard Life Among the Indians
May 1743

David felt like his back was breaking in half. "Lift, John!" he yelled to his sidekick and interpreter friend. The two men lifted up the branchless tree trunk almost six meters long and laid it on top of the stack below it—creating a wall of tree trunks from the ground.

"Whew! How about some water?" David said, wiping the sweat from his forehead with his shirt sleeve.

"Sounds good to me!" John immediately ran into the village and dipped a wooden bowl into a pool of rainwater, which was collected for drinking, and brought it back to David. "Here you are, sir."

"Thank you, John." David looked at their progress and leaned forward on the wall sipping the refreshingly cool water. "I have a long way to go, my friend, but this shall be a good home among your people—a people I have grown to love."

Brainerd glanced at John and then pointed to a stump a few feet away. "Have a sit with me and let us pray together. I need to spend some time with my Lord and would love some company."

John Wauwaumpequnnaunt had been instructed in the Christian religion by John Sergeant and eventually became proficient both in speaking and writing English. He was sent to assist David in his missionary work among the Kaunaumeek Indians.

During the first part of May 1743, David began building a small log cottage for himself next to the Kaunaumeek camp, which was considerably closer than where he had been living for the past two months—almost two miles away with a Scottish family who only spoke Gaelic. Moreover, he enjoyed very little time alone to study and pray while living with this family, which caused considerable grief to David's soul. Sitting down, the two bowed their heads in prayer:

"Heavenly Father, make this home we are building a refuge for the weary and a place of study and prayer so as to further your gospel here among my people."

David now referred to the Kaunaumeek as "my people." They had become very dear to his heart in a short period of time.

His current living conditions were harsh. The family with whom he was staying put him up in a small, one-room cabin next to their home. He had little food, mainly eating boiled corn and small loaves of bread baked in ashes. He slept on a heap of straw thrown over a row of boards. Earlier in March, the straw actually provided considerable warmth, though by the morning, it would be pressed down to a thin layer—not exactly the most comfortable mattress!

For two months, David hadn't spoken with or even seen another English person. Even though John (his interpreter) was a Christian, he was still Indian and part of his own people. Thus, David felt utterly alone with no companion to whom he might lay open his sorrows or take counsel in conversation. Sometimes, he just wanted to talk about how his ministry with the Indians was going. He often felt discouraged and lacked the privilege of having a companion to encourage him to keep pressing on.

Despite the hardships, David desired to be content in his circumstances. He wanted to find true satisfaction in life in knowing his blessed Savior, Jesus Christ. While David throughout the course of his life would wrestle with his own sin and unfitness for ministry, he took refuge in the grace of God in preserving his life. This, it seemed to David, was his great motivation for sharing that same grace with the lost Indians of Kaunaumeek.

* * *

David couldn't see anything! It was pitch black and the call of owls and coyote howls pierced the darkness.

"I cannot be too far from the trail," David said to himself. He turned his horse back around and headed in the direction from which he came—hoping to make his way at least onto the narrow horse trail. All he could find, though, was more trees, more briar patches, and louder howls.

He had been riding from New Haven to Kaunaumeek on a trail he had been on several times, but riding at night was a bit harder. He was hoping the clouds would disperse so that the moon would grant him light, but they showed no signs of clearing. He was lost and alone. What made matters worse was that he didn't have any kind of bedding with him. He had a morsel of bread and an apple a friend had given him in New Haven.

After turning in circles for some time, he stopped and dismounted his horse. "This should be a decent place to rest for the night," he thought, padding down some moss and leaves. He wrapped a rope from his horse around a nearby tree and lay down, fluffing up some extra moss under his head. "This isn't ideal, but it will have to work for tonight. I just hope I can find my way out tomorrow!"

Even though he was completely lost, alone and dark, he was excited about the future. The week prior, on 30th May, he had traveled to New York to request permission to start a school in Kaunaumeek among the Indians—with John serving as the school's first headmaster. The reason why a school was so important, was that the Indians really did want to learn the language of the "white man." They knew it could help their relations as well as provide opportunity for potential business deals in the future. David knew that starting a school would not only help them learn English, but that it would be a place where the Indians could learn about the gospel!

After receiving their approval for the school, he rode to New Haven to try to reconcile some relationships with Yale's authorities. Unfortunately, those same officials who had expelled him were still bitter over the incident and his appeals for reconciliation fell on deaf ears.

Suddenly, the howling shot through the night air making a loud "awooooo" sound. His heart immediately began to pound in his chest and he felt himself nestling lower into his makeshift mossy bed. Although at times he didn't mind dying, being eaten by a wild animal was different!

"I will trust and not be afraid!" he prayed. "I will trust and not be afraid, for you, O Lord, are watching over me. I will trust and not be afraid." He kept repeating to himself over and over until his eyes began to feel heavy. Though he tossed and turned through the night, he did get some sleep. When the faintest trace of sunlight glowed above the tree line, he got up, saddled his horse and headed back over the nearest hill—eventually finding the trail leading to Kaunaumeek!

The timing couldn't have been better for it was Sunday morning and the Indians were gathering to hear him preach, which had been his custom since he arrived. He had been preparing the week prior so he was ready. To his surprise and despite the fact that he had spent the night in the open air, he felt that he had greater assistance from God in his preaching than ever before! This Lord's Day was indeed a blessing from God.

Sundays were special to New Englanders: it was the Lord's Day. It was taken, in part, from the Old Testament idea of a "Sabbath"—meaning rest—but changed to Sunday because that was the day that Jesus rose from the dead. Moreover, the earliest apostles met together to worship on Sunday. When the Ten Commandments spoke of "remembering the Sabbath," David and most people of his day believed that to be Sunday—the Christian Sabbath. The day was to be spent in worship, preaching of the Bible, prayer, and visiting those who were sick.

On July 31st, 1743, David moved into his little cottage he had started in May. Almost immediately, his typical downcast and depressed heart was lifted and he felt spiritual benefit from his new arrangement.

While living with the Scottish couple nearly two miles away, he spent much of his day traveling back and forth to Kaunaumeek. Now, living among the Indians, he was able to teach every morning and evening. Not only that, he was able to retreat to his cottage for study and prayer in between. David loved life and loved being so close to his people. After four dark and discouraging months, the clouds dissipated and his outlook on ministry there improved.

But as soon as he began taking strides of joy in his work, he was hit with illness—causing him to be confined to his bed. "It might have been the corn," he thought to himself. "Then again, the bread was fairly moldy."

David had been traveling nearly fifteen miles just to get bread. And when he arrived at a nearby village, the only bread he could afford would be moldy. More than this, finding food for his horse was a constant burden and strain on his time and energy. He needed his horse for travel, but the upkeep was difficult.

As he lay on his bed, sharp pains would come and go in his chest when he breathed and he frequently suffered from fever. Some of his new Indian friends brought moist cloths to cool his face, but they were afraid of his disease so they didn't stay. He hadn't coughed up blood in a while, but the pain was similar.

After resting for a couple of weeks, David began to regain his strength. More and more, thoughts of reconciling relationships back in New Haven surfaced in his mind. The next day, August 29th, he saddled up and rode to New Haven, confident that he would find grace from Yale's officials, but he would have never expected what happened ...

* * *

With Yale's graduation commencement ceremony over, David found a nearby tree and sat down with his journal and pen:

"Wednesday September 14th. This day I ought to have taken my degree; but God sees fit to deny it me. And though I was greatly afraid of being overwhelmed with perplexity and confusion, when I should see my classmates take theirs; yet, in the very season of it, God enabled me with calmness and resignation to say, 'The will of the Lord be done' (Acts 21:14)."

He still wanted his record cleared of his expulsion and earlier conflict with the school's officials, but didn't know how to go about it. The last meeting didn't work out so well.

Earlier that day, he had met Jonathan Edwards—a man whom he had heard give a commencement address two years prior, while David was still in school at Yale. He had also heard that he was a gifted preacher, writer and even guide. After thinking for a while under that tree, he resolved to meet with Edwards for direction and guidance over what he should do.

After talking with him and Aaron Burr that evening, David set out to write a full written apology to Rector Clap and the college trustees, asking forgiveness for any wrongdoing he had committed against them. The following day (on Thursday) he submitted the letter, which was detailed in the accounts that took place while he was a student. He really did want to be reconciled, not because he thought it would advance him in any way, but simply because he felt guilty over what he had done.

That aside, he did want to be granted a degree. He believed possessing a degree would tend to his being more extensively useful. The Scottish Society, who was sponsoring David's work among the Kaunaumeek

Indians, sent Aaron Burr as a representative to appeal with Yale officials on Brainerd's behalf—asking to grant David a degree. While the governors of the school were willing to formally accept his letter of apology and even to re-admit him as a student, they were not willing to give him a degree until he completed at least one more year of studies at the college.

The Society did not feel that Brainerd should leave his missionary work to which God had called him in order to return to Yale, so David never graduated or received a degree.

After traveling for several weeks, preaching from town to town, he finally arrived back at Kaunaumeek. Writing again in his journal, he expressed his delight to be "back":

"Tuesday, October 4th. This day rode home to my own house and people. The poor Indians appeared very glad of my return. Found my house and all things in safety. I presently fell on my knees and blessed God for my safe return after a long and tedious journey, and a season of sickness in several places. Blessed be God that has preserved me!"

Over the next several months, he focused his morning and evening teaching time among the Indians on two central themes. First, he taught them about their sinful hearts and minds and how they were in bondage—as with chains—to their sin. Moreover, that sin was to be judged by God Almighty, the King of the universe, because it was ultimately rebellion against him! This was the "bad" news.

The second theme he taught them was the "good" news, the gospel. He taught them that because God so loved the world, he gave his only and eternal Son, Jesus Christ. Jesus was born in a manger as a baby, but was fully God and fully human at the same time. He lived a life of perfect obedience to all of God's commandments— never sinning even once! And, as was planned and foretold by the Old Testament prophets, Jesus suffered the pain of being mocked, beaten, whipped, and crucified on a cross. He did this all to pay the penalty for our sin. The punishment for sin is death and Jesus paid it by dying in our place. This was the second theme David taught and he called the Indians, week by week, to receive Jesus as their Savior and Lord by simply believing that he lived and died for them.

Brainerd then began, with the help of John his interpreter, composing various prayers related to the Indians' circumstances in their own language— Algonquian. Eventually, he started translating certain Psalms into their language as well, which they would use in singing in Sunday worship. After teaching the basics of the gospel week after week, he thought it would be a good idea to teach an overview of the Bible, beginning in Genesis and going all the way through the New Testament.

In addition to David teaching the Bible, John Wauwaumpequunnaunt taught the newly-established school—teaching children to read and write in English. Brainerd frequently visited the school to exhort the children and teenagers with truths from Scripture in English, suited to their age.

Then, on the evening of Sunday, October 16th, while David was teaching Psalms to the Indians, he suddenly heard a horse quickly riding toward him from the woods.

"Who is that?" David called. But no answer. The sound of the horse's pounding hooves grew louder until a rider appeared from the side of one of the Indian's wigwams.

"Mr David Brainerd!" the rider called, seeming rather frantic. David knew this couldn't be good— nobody was supposed to ride on Sundays! It was the Lord's Day.

Brainerd stepped off a small platform and shouted back. "I am here, sir. What is your business this Lord's Day?"

"May I speak to you in private, sir?"

David panicked a little. "Was it a friend or even a family member who was ill or who had died?" he thought to himself.

The two men walked over to his cottage and David lit a few candles on a small wooden table. "What is it?"

"Read this," the man said, handing David a letter. Opening it quickly, David stretched the sheet out near the candle so as to read its contents:

"Sir, just now we received advice from Col. Stoddard, that there is the utmost danger of a rupture with France. He has received the same from His Excellency our governor, ordering him to give notice to all the exposed places, that they may secure themselves the best they can against any sudden invasion. We thought best to send directly to Kaunaumeek, that you may take prudent measures for your safety that dwell there."

David folded the letter up and stared at the nearby wall. "I think, good sir, that France and Britain will be at war over this territory soon. Other Indians, who are friends with the French, may even attack us here in Kaunaumeek. But there is nothing I can do about it. These events are in God's hands and I am but his servant—called to labor among my people here."

David stood up and shook hands with the messenger. "Tell your governor, thank you for me. I shall ride to Stockbridge the day after tomorrow to gather more information. In the meantime, Godspeed to you." The messenger quickly walked out, jumped on his horse and rode off into the evening.

Winter was quickly approaching. The leaves had already left their home on the trees and David didn't look forward to the harsh temperatures ahead. Along with the November air came a deeper resolve in his mission among the Indians—despite the increased danger. Life was harsh on the frontier and David seemed to feel every bit of it. But in his hardship, he could rest in a peace that surpassed all human understanding. He was loved and he had a heavenly home—ready to welcome him on the other side of death. But it was not yet his time. God still had plans for David that were beyond his imagination.

A New Call to the Frontier!
December 1743

The blistering cold air was relentless. Snow piled along the trail leading from Kaunaumeek to Stockbridge and David was desperately trying to protect his face—especially his nose—from the frigid December wind. Every now and then, snow and ice from the overhanging trees would fall and land in his collar—melting into cold water that would then seep down his back. "Burrr!" David yelped with a jolting shiver.

As he made his way along on his horse, he thought about the warm fire and hot tea awaiting him at John Sergeant's house, who was the pastor in Stockbridge. Just the thought made him feel warm inside. "Ah, that will be so nice to sit with my Bible and journal next to Rev. Sergeant's fire!" he whispered out loud. "And to converse with my friend about serving Jesus … and to pray with him!" He could hardly wait and wanted to just step up his gait into an all-out canter, but knew that was a risky and dangerous move—especially in the slippery snow. He had only ten miles to go, which was still quite a trek. But he was determined and was even giddy with excitement.

The trail winded along the bank of a small river, which was partly covered by ice; only the middle of it was still flowing. As he peered into the dark cold water, he kept dreaming of being at Sergeant's home: "It will be so nice to have a cup of—"

"Whoa, there!" he yelled at his horse. He pulled up on the reigns trying to steady the horse which suddenly started to lose its footing on the snow and ice. "Steady, girl!" he called again, pulling the reins straight up so as to stop the horse from moving completely. But it was too late! The horse had completely lost all bearing of traction on the unstable powder and it reared up on its hind legs—throwing David off the back, through the air and head first into the icy cold river below!

The immediate sensation of freezing water suctioning around his body caused him to instantly lose his breath and break into a state of panic. He clamored and clawed his way to the side and onto the snowy bank, breathing deeply and shaking. He knew he didn't have long before he would go into hypothermia and die. He scrambled up the small hill leading to his horse, which was now just watching its wet rider struggle, and climbed on. "Hayah!" David yelled, kicking the sides of the horse. The two sprinted the rest of the way to Stockbridge. The awaiting fire was no longer simply a nice comfort, but now necessary to his survival.

Throughout the course of the winter of 1743-44, David traveled many times between Kaunaumeek and other towns—preaching, writing, studying, and praying. During January, he wrote to his youngest brother, Israel, exhorting him in the Christian faith:

Be careful to make a good improvement of precious time. When you cease from labor, fill up your time in reading, meditation, and prayer: And while your hands are laboring, let your heart be employed as much as possible in divine thoughts.

Toward the beginning of February, he even began to write a short book, an allegory of the Christian life. The overarching theme of this devotional booklet is that the human heart cannot find satisfaction and happiness in the creation, but only in the Creator—God himself!

As the winter faded into the spring of 1744, God began tugging on David's heart to begin a new journey into the unknown. At that point, he didn't know where God was leading him, but he did know that it was away from his people at Kaunaumeek.

* * *

The Indians pleaded with David to stay. "But who will look after our souls and teach us the way of Christ week by week?"

"There are other fine ministers of the gospel nearby who can travel and preach here. But elsewhere, other Indian tribes have nobody. They need someone to go and to tell them of their sin and their separation from God."

One of the younger Indian men spoke up from the crowd. "But those Indians that you want to go and preach to are not willing to become Christians as we are. They will not listen to you as we have. Therefore, you should stay with us."

David felt that he was getting nowhere in his argument. "Listen, my people of Kaunaumeek. I would like to advise you, then, to re-locate to Stockbridge. There, you will not only have land supplied for you, but you will also have the privilege of learning and growing in God's grace under the shepherding care of Rev. John Sergeant."

At this, the people stopped arguing back and seemed to even like the idea. Besides, life would be easier with all of the amenities and tools the "white man" possessed.

The next day, Sunday, March 11th, David preached his final sermon at Kaunaumeek on the parable of the sower in Matthew 13.

"Be not like the seeds that fell along the path, which were devoured. Be not like the seeds that fell on rocky ground, which were scorched. Be not like seeds that fell among thorns, which were choked out. Rather, my friends of Kaunaumeek, be like the seeds that fell on good soil and produced good fruit. Hear the Word of God, understand what it says and bear Christian fruit—love, joy, peace, patience and the like—which glorify God in heaven."

After addressing the Indians, he packed up his things and started out on a journey that would eventually take him to New Jersey for a meeting with the Scottish Society Commissioners. On his way, however, he was met by a messenger from East Hampton, the town where he had labored for a while before going to Kaunaumeek. The messenger informed David that East Hampton had voted unanimously to invite and accept him as their permanent pastor! David was stunned and greatly humbled by the offer. At the time when he felt that he needed to leave his work among the Kaunaumeek, he was now being offered a nice position as the town's principle pastor!

East Hampton would provide David with all of the luxuries and privileges a town of that day could offer. According to Jonathan Edwards, East Hampton was the fairest, most pleasant town on the whole island, and one of the largest and most wealthy parishes. The people eagerly wanted Brainerd to accept their offer and come as their new pastor. Not knowing what to do, he kept pushing toward New Jersey—committing the whole matter to God in prayer.

On Friday, March 16th, he traveled to Salisbury, where he was detained for a few days due to heavy rain. While in Salisbury, he was met by another messenger; this time from a town called Millington, which was only eight miles from his hometown of Haddam. The letter was sent by the Christian congregation of that town, inviting him to come and be their pastor. David was at a loss for words. "How could two towns both offer invitations to be their pastor in a week?" he thought to himself. The appeal of going to Millington was that it was close to his family in Haddam. Like before, he didn't know what to do. So he committed the matter, once again, to God in prayer:

"Heavenly Father, you know my heart and how I am torn between what I want and what you want. I earnestly seek your will for my life and to not be swayed by earthly comforts. May I never seek to worship the creation above the Creator! Please grant your servant wisdom."

David continued to ride slowly toward New Jersey, stopping due to ill health and to preach at several churches along the way. He finally reached Elizabethtown, then the capital of New Jersey, on the last day of March. On April 5th, he met with the Scottish Society Commissioners who determined that Brainerd should begin a ministry among the Indians along the Delaware River in Pennsylvania and encouraged him to leave as soon as possible.

Now with three options of ministry—the church in East Hampton, the church in Millington and now the new mission among the Indians at the Forks of the Delaware River—David had to make a choice. After much prayer, he chose the hardest option: a new mission among the Indians in Pennsylvania.

Before making the long journey to the Delaware River, he visited friends and family in Haddam and then in Stockbridge. To his surprise, when he arrived in Stockbridge, he saw his people—the Kaunaumeek settling there! They had taken his advice to re-locate and sit under the preaching of John Sergeant. To his great delight, he was able to see them once more, though constantly feeling the pangs of sickness, fever and coughing up blood. His ill health laid him up in Stockbridge for a few more days until he regained his strength.

During the first week in March, he began his journey westward into the wilderness—alone and full of apprehension as to what awaited him. Every day could be his last. Being alone in a vast land of forest, with no protection, little food and continually exposed to the variation of weather, made such a journey extremely dangerous. On top of that, there was constant threat of attack from various Indian tribes, the French or just thieves along the way. On his way, he constantly felt waves of fatigue and weakness, fever and breathing pains. Many times, he would cough up blood—a tell-tale sign of tuberculosis. There was nobody to help him in the wilderness, no doctors and certainly no medicine. Indeed, David had to completely trust that God would provide for him and take care of him along the way.

After riding nearly eighty miles over the course of several days through the thick forest, sleeping when he got the chance, he came upon an Indian village at Minisink. The natives—called the Munsees—were made up of remnants of various ancient Indian tribes. Filled with boldness and courage (not knowing if these Indians would be peaceful or not), David dismounted and walked into the village.

"Greetings!" he called out generally to the Indians who were now looking at him with great suspicion. Nobody answered. He wasn't sure if anyone spoke English, but he kept on anyway. "I would like to speak to your chief. I come here in the name of the Lord Jesus Christ and to teach of his ways."

"I am he," a deep voice thundered from behind a growing wall of people.

David was relieved that he knew at least some English! "May I speak with you alone?" he asked trying to peer through the crowd to find the man.

As the crowd parted, a large older man with long dark hair appeared—motioning with his hand for David to follow him. David immediately dropped the leather strap on his horse and walked after the man into a mid-sized wigwam with a smoldering fire near its doorway.

He looked around the home, which was furnished with various animal skins and pottery, somewhat fascinated with the care and detail of the tools and inscriptions.

"I have heard of your Jesus and people like you who call themselves Christians. We do not want anything to do with you or your God!"

David didn't know what to say. "What do you mean?"

The chief seemed to be rather annoyed by David's presence. "Why do you desire us to become Christians when I have seen these so-called Christians acting much worse than Indians naturally do? The Christians lie, steal and drink worse than the Indians. It is they who have brought such drunkenness to our village!"

An overwhelming sadness and disappointment came over David and he felt ashamed for what people had done in the name of Jesus Christ. "I condemn all conduct of these people who are called Christians, sir. That is not the way of Christ and I am sorry you have witnessed such sorry living."

David apologized over and over and implored the chief not to think of true Christianity in such a negative way. Over the course of half an hour, the chief seemed to listen to what David was telling him about the way of Jesus and how the Savior can free a man's soul in this life and in the one to come. Though the chief didn't accept Jesus as his Savior, he was willing to hear from David again on these matters. After resting there for the night, he packed up and continued on south and west.

Finally, on May 12th, he arrived at Hunter's Settlement, which was twelve miles above the Forks of the Delaware. The Forks is located at the confluence of the Delaware and Lehigh Rivers. The hundred miles of forest and mountains that Brainerd had crossed was a desolate and hideous country, with very few settlements. But he made it and was welcomed by Alexander Hunter, who had established Hunter's Settlement.

Alexander was the leader of a group of Scots-Irish families who settled there fifteen years prior and owned over 300 acres of land. He operated a ferry across the Delaware and was known as a well-educated and pious man. He was happy to host David as the town's new missionary.

David, however, wasn't quite so happy. During his first full day there, which happened to be Sunday—the Lord's Day—he noticed children frolicking around and adults talking about vain things with no regard for God or heaven. He was also disappointed that there was not a suitable interpreter for his needs. The Indians whom he was hoping to evangelize were scattered and the whole situation was much bleaker than he had anticipated.

Hunter's Settlement had no church building, but had been visited by a number of men whom David knew: Eleazar Wales, Gilbert Tennent, Charles Beatty, Azariah Horton and Charles McKnight. While these men did a good service in visiting and preaching at Hunter's Settlement, there was not a permanent pastor to shepherd the people there.

On May 17th, almost a week after he had arrived, he met with the local Indians by appointment and preached to them. They were very open to hear his message and even their chief wanted him to continue—even using his own home to do so, which was about three miles down from Hunter's Settlement! Even though the number of Indians in the entire area near the Forks was small, God was pleased to give David this encouraging welcome from the start.

Most of the Indians who used to live in the area had already moved further westward into the Pennsylvania wilderness. Only about ten Indian families remained. At one time, however, it was a thriving Indian community of hundreds of people, living in well-constructed homes. However, through the ever-expanding settlements of the English, the natives' cultural life had largely disappeared. More and more of them took on the English culture. Those who wanted to preserve their native identity and customs moved west.

After only two weeks of being at Hunter's Settlement, Brainerd received word from the New York presbytery, which met in Newark, New Jersey, that he was to be examined for ordination. "Ordination!" David was thrilled. Yet, he was also scared of the thought—that he, such a vile and worthless sinner would be called into the life long ministry and calling of God.

He at once packed his things for the journey back and, on Monday, May 28th, left for New Jersey. In a few short days, he had made the long trek back to Elizabethtown where he finalized his study and preparations for the examinations. A week later, on June 11th, Brainerd preached on an assigned text from Acts 26:17-18:

"Delivering thee from the people, and from the Gentiles, unto whom now I send thee, to open their eyes, and to turn them from darkness to light, and from the power of Satan unto God, that they may receive forgiveness of sins, and inheritance among them which are sanctified by faith that is in me."

After the sermon was finished, David was examined in areas of theology, doctrine, biblical knowledge and his Christian experience. Having satisfactorily passed all the examinations, he was ordained on June 12th, 1744 to the gospel ministry. This meant that he was a full-fledged "Reverend" and gospel minister. He was authorized to administer the sacraments and to be called as a permanent pastor.

But along with all of the privileges given to David, he also felt an overwhelming sense of the responsibility such an office held. Reflecting in his journal that day, he wrote:

"Oh, that I might always be engaged in the service of God, and duly remember the solemn charge I have received, in the presence of God, angels, and men; Amen!"

Now ordained, he had a mission awaiting him at the Forks of the Delaware. God had qualified him internally and, now, externally through the presbytery to preach the gospel of Jesus Christ to the lost and broken of this world—the lost and broken at the edge of the frontier wilderness.

The Ground Breaks Open
Summer 1744

After David's ordination, on Saturday June 19th, he rode for three days back to the Forks of the Delaware—back to Hunter's Settlement. When he arrived, he immediately set out to translate some of the biblical prayers into the Indian language with the help of a new interpreter, Moses Tattamy.

Tattamy had served as a translator for the Penn government in Pennsylvania and greatly admired the English way of life, even encouraging his fellow natives to embrace the English customs and laws. Although he was somewhat acquainted with Christianity, Moses Tattamy was not a Christian—a fact that would prove difficult in working with Brainerd. But David was thankful to have an interpreter to help him to preach to the lost Indians around Hunter's Settlement.

On the Lord's Day, June 29th, David and Moses rode several miles down the Delaware River to preach to the Indian village. During his morning sermon, his mind kept wandering off so that he could hardly focus his attention on what he was saying. This brought David great inner distress so that he felt that he was preaching without heart.

However, God began to prepare him to preach like he'd never preached before. With the Indians gathered around and Moses to his side, he opened up the Bible to Jeremiah 10:2, 3 and read:

"Thus saith the LORD, 'Learn not the way of the heathen and be not dismayed at the signs of heaven; for the heathen are dismayed at them. For the customs of the people are vain'."

For the next two hours, he pleaded with the natives to turn from all the vanities and idols of this world and embrace the true and living God. All of the sudden—to David's great joy—the Indians began to cry out with tears of conviction and they were more attentive to what David was saying than they had ever been before.

He spent the rest of the evening praying to God, thanking him for His great work among the Indians. He wrote in his journal later that week on July 6th, that "of late all my concern almost is for the conversion of the heathen; and for that end I long to live." Indeed, he longed to have less and less of a desire for all the pleasures this world has to offer and to be filled with the grace and pleasures granted by God in Christ Jesus. David was seeing the first signs of the ground breaking open—Indians beginning to embrace Christianity.

However, these first fruits of David's missionary labors were met by a wall of ancient Indian belief and custom—a worship of satanic powers and gods in a wild dance and feast. He received news of an event on

July 21st and quickly retreated into the woods to pour out his heart to God:

"Heavenly Father, I know they are meeting together to worship devils and not you, the true and living God. Would you now appear and help my attempts to break up this idolatrous meeting and convict their sinful hearts—turning them toward your promises of grace and mercy found only through faith in Christ Jesus?"

He was so burdened for the Indians souls, that during his prayer, he poured out sweat and tears before his God. He could hardly sleep through the night, knowing that he was about to ride into a worship ceremony of Satan.

The next morning, he got up, saddled his horse and set off with his interpreter three miles to where the Indians were meeting—continually asking God for his presence and assistance. The morning was cool and David had an inner peace that he was doing the right thing.

As he approached, he heard drums and loud chanting. The smoke from a great fire created a dark cloud above the trees ahead. "Lord, grant me courage!" he prayed before breaking through the last row of trees. The Indians were all dancing around in a circle and seemed as if they were controlled by demons or some other evil spirit. They didn't even notice him ride up, but then—

"Hello, people of the Delaware!" he shouted with a timidity in his voice.

The drums came to a sudden halt and the whole village turned to look upon the missionary. David felt a twinge of fear, but took a deep breath. "I desperately need to speak with you this day—morning and evening about this dance and feast. It is displeasing in the sight of God Almighty and I plead with you to listen to what I have to say."

The Indians looked at one another and to David's surprise put down the drums and removed some of the festive clothing. David and his interpreter jumped off their horses and walked toward the crowd and for the whole day preached to them from God's Word. God had used him to break up their assembly and listen to his message of peace and love found in Jesus Christ.

For the remainder of the summer of 1744, God assisted David's preaching ministry among the Indians so that the weekly attendees of his sermons grew from less than twenty to nearly fifty! He knew this was only the work of God. His task was to plant and water the gospel; God provided the growth in peoples' hearts.

* * *

"Please, Eliab, come with me to Susquehanna!" David said with utmost earnestness.

The young minister really did seem to want to go with David. "I would love to, but my congregation needs me here in Rockciticus. Perhaps at another date?"

"I think it would do both of us good to spend some time together in ministry. Besides, you need some time away from your church here."

Eliab stood up and walked over to his desk, looking down at an old leather Bible. "Alright, David. I will join you." He picked up the Bible, and turned, looking at David with a big grin: "You and I will travel to Susquehanna in the morning and preach to the Indians. May God be with us, encourage our hearts and apply his holy Word to the Indians there!"

Eliab Byram, a 1740 Harvard graduate, was the pastor of the Presbyterian Church in Rockciticus, New Jersey, which was about twenty-seven miles east of Hunter's Settlement. It was on the way toward Susquehanna. During the month of September, David had made a three-week journey to New England to obtain permission from the Scottish Society to minister to the Indians living at the Susquehanna River. After receiving permission, he rode back to Hunter's Settlement to make preparations for the trip.

Ministry was often a lonely endeavor for Brainerd. Many times, he felt that he was the only one seeking to win the hearts of people toward a relationship with God. He knew other ministers shared the struggle, but his contact with them was so limited. Here he lived, on the edge of the western frontier, in the woods at a small English settlement adjacent to an Indian village. It was not the ideal life people dreamed of, rather it was full of constant danger, little food, continual exposure to harsh weather, and threat of attack from nearby bands of raiding Indians. But, this was the life God had called him to and it was in such a call that David found his great purpose.

The following day, on October 2nd, David, Eliab, and two Indians from the village near Hunter's Settlement set out on a twenty-five mile journey to the Susquehanna River. That evening, they lodged at one of the last houses along that road before entering into what Brainerd later described as "a hideous and howling wilderness."

The next day, they found themselves traveling in a most difficult terrain—steep mountains, deep valleys, and treacherous rocks. Earlier travelers along this certain road would often use ropes to attach themselves to one another, so as to not fall off various cliffs along this western portion of the Appalachian mountain range.

Late in the afternoon, as they rode along, they came upon a steep and rocky incline. David began slowly up the side of the mountain, his horse struggling to keep balance. All of a sudden, his horse buckled underneath him—sending David tumbling down the steep slope. After rolling to a stop, David quickly checked his hands and body for any serious injuries. Having an injury thirty miles from the closest house could prove deadly.

Seeing none, he looked back up the hill to find his horse shaking violently on the ground and writhing in pain. He scrambled up the hill, back toward it. Eliab had already dismounted to look at David's horse.

"Can you see what is wrong?" David called out, still climbing up the bank.

Eliab looked closely at the horse's leg, which was all mangled and twisted. "I think I have some very bad news."

Huffing and puffing, David reached his horse and saw for himself. The reason his horse buckled beneath him was that its leg got caught between two rocks and broke. He knew what this meant. There was no way to fix his horse's leg out here in the middle of the wilderness—he was going to have to shoot it.

The thought of having to kill his horse was painful. She had been his faithful mare for nearly five thousand miles. Indeed, he felt a close connection with this companion in ministry.

"I'm sorry, David," Eliab said pulling a rifle out from a side pouch on his own horse. "Do you want me to do it?"

David couldn't believe what was happening, but took a deep breath and took the rifle from Eliab. With the deed done, he turned to his fellow travelers and spoke with resolve: "God is faithful and good. He will get us through this wilderness and to the Susquehanna." One of the Indians jumped off his horse and told David he would walk the rest of the way. But David refused, having already made up his mind that he would do the walking.

The small band continued on until they finally reached the Indian settlement called Opeholhaupung on Friday, October 5th—on the Susquehanna River. The village composed of about seventy Indians living in a dozen or so native houses. After greeting the local Indian chief in a warm fashion, he told him of his desire to teach them about Jesus Christ.

With interest, the chief agreed and the men of the village began to assemble to hear Brainerd preach and teach about the truth of the gospel. He addressed them twice that day and at noon the next.

The Indian men had planned a hunting expedition, but agreed to delay the trip in order to hear more of Brainerd's teaching that Sunday. On the Lord's Day, with the Indians gathered together, David preached with power and freedom. Many seemed very attentive and some felt convicted by what he said. However, for the first time, his message was immediately met with strong objections from some.

One of the main objections against Christianity from the natives there was that they had witnessed the vicious lives and un-Christian behavior of certain so-called "Christians" in the past. They were poor examples of Christianity and had left a sour taste in the mouths of these Indians. David pleaded with them that that was not the conduct of a true believer in Jesus and apologized for such an experience.

Another objection against embracing Christianity was their own customs, traditions and pagan religion, which had been passed down through the generations in their tribe. Moreover, the Indians were fearful of their own witchdoctors, whom they called

"Powwows". These Powwows apparently possessed powers of enchanting, or poisoning people to death and the Indians feared what might happen to them if they turned from their religion to embrace the saving grace found in the gospel.

While David understood their position, he told them of the greater danger of not trusting in Christ— that he alone was the true Judge of the living and the dead and apart from a saving relationship with him, they would experience everlasting torment in hell.

While none of the Indians committed their lives to Jesus that day, the chief welcomed Brainerd to come again to teach them—an invitation he was very encouraged to hear!

Along the way back to Hunter's Settlement, they stopped at another small settlement to obtain a new horse for David. Though it wasn't like his former faithful steed, this one would be his new companion in future ministry. After arriving back at the Forks, he took out his journal and praised God for his provision:

"Friday, October 12th. Rode home to my lodging; where I poured out my soul to God in secret prayer, and endeavored to bless him for his abundant goodness to me in my late journey. God marvelously, and almost miraculously, supported me under the fatigues of the way, and traveling on foot. Blessed be the Lord, that continually preserves me in all my ways."

* * *

Up until now, David had been living with Alexander Hunter, the founder of Hunter's Settlement. But by the end of November, a few other members of the Settlement decided to construct a small cottage for David to live in. So they began the building of David's residence during the first snowy days of December.

The cottage wasn't anything fancy, but it was sturdy and a perfect place for David to retreat for private prayer and study, which were the source of his motivation and energy for enduring ministry among the Indians. Ministers of the gospel find great delight in coming to God's Word after being in steady ministry. As the Psalmist writes in Psalm 42: "As the deer panteth after water brooks, so panteth my soul after thee, O God."

On December 9th, he crossed the Delaware River and preached twice at Greenwich, New Jersey— about ten miles from his new cottage. While he preached, he was so filled with affection and desire for Jesus, that during the middle of his sermon, tears streamed down his cheeks. All who heard were greatly affected by his preaching. In fact, one individual who was present absolutely shocked David that day, Moses Tattamy!

Tattamy had been David's constant interpreter while serving at Hunter's Settlement and, while helpful, proved to lack the saving faith he was speaking about to his fellow natives. But on that day, God would take hold of Moses' heart and give him a new heart of loving faith. After his sermon, Moses took David aside and explained what was happening.

"I am in a miserable and perishing condition, David," Tattamy said trying to hold back his tears. "I see plainly what I have been doing all my days, and I have never done one good thing. I have done many things that folks call good—I have been kind to my neighbors. But all of these things have not come from a heart of faith or of love for God. I want to turn and trust in Jesus to save my soul."

David was thrilled and from that day, began noticing a change in Moses' character and attitude. He was a new man; the old was gone and, behold, the new had come! David preached again to the people at Greenwich, with Moses at his side interpreting to the Indians, but this time—more than ever—they experienced the power of the Spirit of God and most of the people in the crowd began weeping over their lost condition and cried out for salvation. David was witnessing the fruit of his labors among the Indians!

Through the remainder of that winter and into the early spring of 1745, David continued to see God's amazing work among those who heard his preaching. Both the English and the Indians had a desire to know more about the living and true God and wanted to understand the depth of the riches of the gospel as found in the Bible.

After preaching at Hunter's Settlement, on February 17th, he found a nearby grove of trees in which to sit and write in his journal:

"I think I was scarce ever enabled to offer the free grace of God to perishing sinners with more freedom and plainness in my life. And afterwards I was enabled earnestly to invite the children of God to come renewedly, and drink of this foundation of water of life, from whence they have heretofore derived unspeakable satisfaction. There were many tears in the assembly; and I doubt not but that the Spirit of God was there, convincing poor sinners of their need of Christ."

Pressing On Toward Exhaustion
Spring 1745

David made plans. Having spent two years in a very solitary ministry—both at Kaunaumeek and at the Forks of the Delaware River, he was tired of being alone in his ministry among the Indians. It was time to recruit a partner in ministry—a colleague who would travel with him and be completely spent for the preaching and ministry of the gospel of Jesus Christ to the natives. While needing time alone with God, Brainerd also needed the company of a fellow Christian minister with whom he could enjoy mutual encouragement and the burden of ministry.

So, on March 6th, 1745, he set out on a five-week journey to New England to find and recruit a ministry companion. He was fully optimistic that somebody would want to join him in a life dedicated in service to Christ on the western frontier. He also intended that this individual—whoever he may be—would accompany him back to the Susquehanna River to evangelize the various native tribes living there.

He didn't have much money—just what the Scottish Society was providing. But when he heard that his friend, John Sergeant, was starting a new mission up near Stockbridge, he sold two tea kettles and some blankets and sent the money to Sergeant. His heart was torn between what to do about money because he knew he needed money to help cover the cost of a new ministry companion as well. But he didn't care about the few possessions that he had. The possibility of God saving souls through Sergeant's mission was more important to him.

Over the course of those five weeks, he tried to find somebody who would journey with him to the Susquehanna River to begin a more permanent mission among the Indians there. To his great frustration, however, after traveling over 600 miles, he returned to the Forks on Saturday, April 13th, with no companion. But despite his disappointment, he thanked God for keeping him safe on his travels and—though he was fatigued and ill—managed to gain enough strength to preach the next day, Easter Sunday, to a sizable assembly of settlers. He preached from Ezekiel 33:11: "Say unto them, 'As I live,' saith the Lord GOD, 'I have no pleasure in the death of the wicked; but that the wicked turn from his way and live'."

No rest for the weary, however! Over the next few days, he rode over fifty miles south to Philadelphia to obtain permission from the Governor and from the Six Nations Confederacy to live along the Susquehanna River in missionary service to the Indians living there.

The Six Nations Confederacy, also known as the Iroquois Confederacy, was made up of five Iroquois tribes from New York and one from North Carolina.

This assembly controlled the entire length of the Susquehanna River. The fact that there were many different Indian tribes that lived along the Susquehanna made the location an ideal mission for preaching the gospel.

After receiving permission, he set out on his journey once more to his little cottage at the Forks—stopping along the way at the home of Charles Beatty, pastor of the Presbyterian Church at Neshaminy. Neshaminy was located about twelve miles north of Philadelphia. Beatty, who was four years older than Brainerd, was a 1742 graduate of a frontier college known as the Log College.

The Log College was a "New Side" college headed by William Tennent, Sr., the father of Gilbert Tennent who was a New Side evangelist who had stirred up some controversy during the recent Great Awakening. Brainerd ended up staying with Beatty a few days and even accompanied him to a town several miles south called Abington to administer the sacrament of the Lord's Supper.

Administering the Lord's Supper, according to the Church of Scotland (under whose authority Brainerd was ministering), was quite unusual to many. The service, which usually lasted five days, began on Thursday—a day set aside for prayer and fasting.

On Thursday, small metal discs were handed out to Christians who were "approved," meaning they exhibited consistent Christian conduct along with their confession of faith. Worship services were held all day on Saturday in preparation for receiving the Lord's Supper on Sunday. They received the Supper seated at tables, where the bread and wine were given to the participants only after they had turned in their metal discs. Psalms were sung and the whole service lasted somewhere between seven or eight hours!

After preaching from Matthew 5:3 and witnessing considerable response from the congregation, he rode back to his cottage at the Forks on April 29th, quite weak and physically sick. But despite his ongoing weakness, he was determined to carry out his plan— even if it meant pushing himself to the brink of absolute exhaustion—of evangelizing the Indians in the Susquehanna region through the summer at least.

On Wednesday, May 8th, he set out toward the Susquehanna with his interpreter, Moses Tattamy. The two were almost giddy with excitement about their adventure. The warm sun seemed to bring an internal glow and comfort about their mission.

Despite their high spirits, thoughts of his last journey into the wilderness between the Forks and Susquehanna with Eliab began to creep into his mind. It wasn't that long ago when the crew had ventured through the rough wilderness and David's horse had broken its leg between two rocks. He missed his old horse and missed Eliab's companionship, but having Moses was a definite encouragement.

Soon, however, dark clouds quenched the warm afternoon sunlight and the two men could see the approaching wall of thick rain up ahead. Before they could think of what to do, a cold northeasterly storm broke over their heads and—not finding an adequate shelter—they decided to press on in hope of finding something to rest under for the night.

If this wasn't bad enough, their horses refused to keep going and seemed rather sick. David realized that when they had stopped to take a break earlier that day, the horses had eaten some bad vegetation. There they were; hiking over rocky terrain in the middle of a raging storm with sick horses. The optimistic spirit that they had setting out fled from the pounding peels of thunder overhead.

At twilight, they stumbled across an abandoned log hut and David was thankful to God for providing shelter for the night. Although everything they had was drenched and they were cold, the two were thankful to be out of the rain.

The next morning, they awoke, squeezed out the remaining moisture from their clothes and rode the rest of the way to the Susquehanna. Over the next few days, they travelled over 100 miles along the river, visiting many different Indian tribes. At each village, they stopped and God was gracious to provide adequate interpreters. David would preach, receiving mixed results. Most objected to the gospel he communicated.

They finally arrived at one of the largest Indian towns in Pennsylvania at the time, Shamokin. Shamokin had nearly 300 natives living in over fifty homes and actually comprised of three separate Indian tribes: the Delewares, the Senecas and the Tutelos. When they rode into Shamokin, Brainerd noticed the number of men drinking liquor and fighting. After only half an hour, he had a good idea of the moral condition of the town and how much these people needed the gospel of Jesus Christ.

After spending a few days, sleeping in the nearby woods, he had a chance to meet with a prominent Iroquois chief, named Shikellamy, who had just been promoted to executive deputy of the Grand Council of the Six Nations Confederacy. Shikellamy commanded the respect of both Indians and Englishmen alike. Intelligent, dignified and refined, his work at bringing peace between the Indians and the English was known throughout New England.

David wanted permission from Shikellamy to live near Shamokin along the banks of the Susquehanna and teach Christianity to the natives. After making known this desire to Shikellamy, the chief gave a resounding "No!" He would not let a missionary stay there. Though he respected the white man, he would not let him try to convert the natives to the white man's religion.

David was heartbroken. He had spent months preparing himself to live among the Indians here and now he was forbidden to do so by the chief! Not knowing what to do, he returned to the nearby woods to find Moses talking with some of the locals. Moses had found them a place to stay for a few days, which was good news; though nothing could have lifted David's spirits at that point.

That night, David became very ill. The tireless riding, preaching and ministering to various people over the last several months had taken their toll on his body. He had passed through considerable hardships— riding in the wilderness, sleeping in the open air, and fatigued by the pressures of ministry. He was seized with a burning fever and felt extreme pains in his head and bowels. More than that, though, he coughed up great amounts of blood. He stayed in an Indian's hut for over a week, trying to gain enough strength to ride.

Finally, the two saddled up and rode back toward the Forks, arriving on May 30th with great disappointment. Brainerd and Tattamy had ridden over 340 miles in twenty-three days and they were exhausted! A letter awaited David asking for his assistance in Neshaminy where Charles Beatty needed help administering another Communion Service. So on Friday, June 7th, he rode the forty-mile journey to Neshaminy where he was greeted by over three thousand people, waiting with eager expectation to receive the elements of the Lord's Supper!

Still weak and somewhat sick, he managed to preach that Sunday on Isaiah 53:10, "Yet it pleased the

LORD to bruise him." His subject was on the sovereign will of God to send forth his only Son, Jesus Christ, to be our perfect substitute on the cross. For the salvation of sinners he preached the next morning on Psalm 17:15, "I shall be satisfied, when I awake, with thy likeness," meditating on the glorified resurrection of our earthly bodies after Christ returns as the Judge of the living and the dead.

After spending some good time with Beatty and some other ministers of the gospel, David pulled out his journal once again and began to write:

"Tuesday, June 11th. Spent the day mainly in conversation with dear Christian friends; and enjoyed some sweet sense of divine things. Oh, how desirable it is to keep company with God's dear children! Oh, what delight will it afford to meet them all in a state of perfection! Lord, prepare me for that state!"

***

Four Indian women sat in a row on a log bench in front of Brainerd. They were his Sunday morning church attendees—the only ones who came to hear him in Crossweeksung, which was a little Indian village in southern New Jersey. After he finished preaching, he looked upon the women with compassion, who seemed to be moved by what David had said.

"If you desire, I shall be here tomorrow to preach again," he said closing his Bible in his hands.

The women all seemed to be greatly pleased with the idea and so David told Moses of the plans. That night, those women traveled some ten to fifteen miles around Crossweeksung to gather others to come and hear Brainerd the next day. And sure enough, they came! This time, there were more than thirty natives who had come out to hear the young preacher. He spent considerable time discussing with them about their sinful condition and the hope of eternal life found through faith in Jesus Christ.

The next Thursday, June 27th, over forty Indians gathered to hear David preach on the riches of the gospel. He wrote in his journal later that day:

"My soul rejoiced to find that God enabled me to be faithful, and that he was pleased to awaken these poor Indians by my means. Oh, how heart-reviving and soul-refreshing is it to me to see the fruit of my labors!"

Although he really enjoyed seeing the fruit of his ministry at Crossweeksung, he had not forgotten about his people back at the Forks of the Delaware. He told the Crossweeksung Indians of his plans to return to the Forks and they pleaded with him to stay.

"Soon," he told them. "I shall try—Lord willing— to return to you as soon as possible to teach you about the Bible and about my God and Savior."

He arrived back at the Hunter's Settlement on July 12th, very weak from preaching and riding. Two days later, he had the great joy and privilege of baptizing his first true converts: Moses Tattamy and his family. They came forward during the worship service and, with many Indians and English assembled, he addressed the crowd:

"The Tattamys have been awakened to a solemn concern for their souls," David began with a strong resolve in his voice. "They have both appeared to be comforted with divine consolations and it is apparent they have passed a great and saving change."

They came forward and knelt down in front of David. He dipped his hand into a basin of water and baptized them "in the name of the Father, and of the Son and of the Holy Spirit."

Baptism, according to the Presbyterian tradition, wasn't just an external observance, but God actually sealed his promises to those being baptized. It was the outward sign of God's grace being sealed to them— pointing to the washing of their sins by the blood of Christ and their newness in the Christian life. The service was closed with David exhorting all who were assembled to examine their own hearts as to whether or not they—internally—had been baptized; that is, had their hearts been washed with the forgiving blood of Christ?

On the last day of July, David once again set out for Crossweeksung, wanting to fulfill his promise that he would return soon. He made the seventy-mile journey in just two days and preached from Revelation 22:17 on August 3rd, "And whosoever will, let him take the water of life freely." A group of Indians formed to hear him and all but two were in tears by the time he had finished—concerned over their eternal destiny. One of the women who had listened fell under such conviction that she embraced Jesus Christ as her Lord and Savior! Where David was planting and watering the gospel, God provided the growth!

But this was only the beginning. God had been preparing, not just individuals to receive his mercy in salvation, but whole peoples. Indeed, the events leading up to and on Thursday, August 8th, 1745 were so remarkable; it could have been nothing but a special outpouring of the Spirit of God upon the people who listened to David's preaching.

* * *

The entire room and those standing outside wept bitterly over their sin and pleaded for God's mercy. Many could barely stand or even sit. Some simply lay on the floor shaking from such strong weeping.

David was preaching from Luke 14:16-23— Jesus' parable of the invitation to the heavenly banquet—and had opened up the gospel's call for sinners to be forgiven by trusting in Jesus – the one who had paid for their sin and died in their place. Some in the room went out and started telling all those around the house about the goodness of Christ and the comfort that is to be enjoyed in him. David was utterly amazed! Young and old, men and women, boys and girls, Indians and English settlers—all fell under a great conviction of their own sin and of God's great love.

This spiritual awakening continued into the next day. David preached that Friday afternoon to more than seventy people, unpacking the parable of the sower from Matthew 13. He preached Saturday, twice on Sunday and throughout the following week. His ministry among the Indians there had such dramatic effect that people from all over were hearing of the awakening happening at Crossweeksung.

David received an invitation to come and preach at William Tennent's church at Freehold, more than twenty miles away. Tennent's church was not only the largest Presbyterian Church in the region, but happened to be the first regularly constituted Presbyterian Church in America! After preaching that Sunday, he returned to Crossweeksung and proceeded to baptize twenty-five Indian converts, exhorting them to remain strong together as a community of Christian faith. The next day, he preached to more than one hundred gathered natives from the gospel of John 6:51-55. His sermon was about how Jesus is the "living bread which came down from heaven."

David's ministry was taking off and all the while he was pressing on toward exhaustion. Could his body keep up with his spirit? Would he be able to continue at such a pace of preaching and traveling and exhorting people from the Word of God?

Toward the end of August 1745, Brainerd was fully convinced that he should take another shot at preaching to the Indians along the Susquehanna River.

With a new-found joy and encouragement from the conversions at Crossweeksung, he set out toward the western frontier.

Preaching morning, afternoon and evening, David labored up and down the Susquehanna until he was completely spent. On one occasion, he nearly fainted from exhaustion! Riding, preaching, visiting Indian homes to pray and minister to families all made up his busy life.

As summer faded into fall, and fall into winter, his pace didn't let up. He was baptizing more people than ever, preaching more than ever, and was always on his horse going to a new town or village. He was wearing himself out in service of Jesus, yet all the while, he felt this was his call and joy and crown. But, while his spirit was willing, his flesh was weak—and growing deathly ill.

A Love for My People

November 1745

David's face grimaced under a sudden writhing chest pain and he bent over in his chair. "Lord, grant me strength!" he prayed under his breath. The thick smoke from the fireplace made his lungs burn like an internal furnace—fanned hotter with every inhale and exhale.

After a few minutes, the pain began to subside and he sat back up, listening in on the rest of the presbytery meeting. The fireplace was on the opposite wall and though most of the smoke funneled up the chimney, a considerable amount puffed out into the large open room. But it was worth being warm!

"Any other business, gentlemen?" the moderator continued with great solemnity, pausing to scan the crowd of ministers from around the area. "Seeing none, I conclude this meeting adjourned until January. May the God of peace, the love of Christ and the fellowship of the Holy Spirit be with you all. Amen."

David needed some fresh air, and fast! Standing up quickly, he made his way toward the door to get his horse—trying not to get "caught" in a conversation on his way out. He finally broke out into the chilly November night, taking several deep cold breaths. The stars shimmered across the sky like twinkling lights and the moon cast a cool glow, across the powdery snow. David still enjoyed some residual heat from the meeting and thanked God for preserving him through so much riding and preaching these past few months.

He turned and walked down the row of horses that lined the front of the meeting house toward the end, but when he got to where his horse was tied, it was gone! He quickly glanced back down the row to make sure he hadn't missed it and then peered down the lantern-lit street: nothing. Somebody had stolen his horse!

He had very little money and could barely afford food for himself. "Heavenly Father," he prayed, looking up into the night sky. "Please grant me wisdom. What shall I do now?" He looked back toward the door. The people were now filing out and talking about the meeting's discussion.

"Excuse me!" David called, walking toward the door.

Several of the men turned toward him and one seemed to look directly at him. "Yes, David. Can I help you?"

"It appears that my horse has been stolen," he said pointing back to the end of the row.

"I'm so sorry. Have you looked around?"

Giving another quick glance up and down the street, he said with a rather unsure tone, "I have … briefly."

"Well, I have an extra horse that I would be willing to sell if you would like, David."

"Sir, I really do not have much money. I am a missionary with the—"

The man came up to David and put his hand on his shoulder. "Don't worry, young Brainerd. Pay what you can and that shall be sufficient."

"Oh, thank you, sir! Thank you!" David really was deeply grateful that God would provide so quickly for his need. He followed the man down the road, turning after a couple of blocks, and entered a rather humble one-story house. The man disappeared for a few minutes and finally returned with a horse.

"Here you are, David. She should suit your travel needs just fine."

After thanking him again, David climbed on the horse and rode toward the ferry house to spend the night. The ferry house was located on the western edge of Newtown, Long Island and provided transportation back and forth to New Jersey. He had been traveling throughout various parts of New Jersey in order to solicit funds for his mission among the Indians. He'd also been trying to recruit a new schoolmaster who could oversee the education of the Crossweeksung natives.

The next day, he set out toward Crossweeksung, stopping by several friends' houses along the way. Since March 1745, he had traveled over three thousand miles, baptized nearly fifty people, and preached on average three to four times a week!

The demanding pace, though, had taken a toll on his health. He constantly suffered from fatigue, fever, and often coughed up blood. At times, he wanted to die due to severe pain in his chest. However, David knew that God had him there for a purpose—to share his amazing grace and love to people who didn't know him. David was ready to die and go to heaven, but many of the Indians were not. He resolved to use every minute he could in the service of Christ.

* * *

As he was riding into Crossweeksung on Saturday, December 7th, he noticed the people glowing with smiles and breaking out with controlled giggles. He got the sense that they knew something he didn't.

He jumped off his horse and greeted his people with a slight grin himself. They had him follow them up to his *new cottage*! "I'm amazed!" he said out loud. He couldn't believe it. While he was gone, the Indians had taken the initiative and built him a small cottage.

"Thank you, thank you, thank you," he told them over and over. He offered up a prayer of thanks to God—again! It was clear that God was looking after his needs, even when at the moment he didn't see how things were going to work out.

The following Saturday, December 14th, David woke up unusually early. He could already hear the crackle of a fire starting outside his cottage and was grateful for the service of his selfless Christian natives.

They were his people—his congregation, which now totaled over 120.

After putting on his thick coat, he thought through his plans for the day and felt that God was pressing him to try something new, something fresh and exciting. He glanced around the rather dark room and looked at his books, which were stacked on a makeshift wooden desk. Scanning the row of titles, he spotted his Westminster Confession of Faith and Catechisms.

"Ah, yes!" he said with an immediate enthusiasm. He walked over, picked up the leather book and opened to the first page of the Westminster Shorter Catechism. He read question number one in an excited whisper. "What is the chief end of man?"

"Man's chief end is to glorify God and to enjoy him forever," he said a little louder, smiling to himself.

The catechism had been written during the English Civil war in the 1640s at Westminster Abbey in London. The ministers and officers from all over England and Scotland originally met to provide the church with official documents of worship. But after much debate, set out to produce an entirely new confession of faith, along with a larger and shorter catechism.

A catechism is simply a document of doctrine in a question-answer format. The purpose was to train the church in theology and sound belief so that, during the sermons on Sunday, the people could receive spiritual "meat," and not just "milk".

David continued to thumb through the pages of his catechism and decided that his new task would be to train his Indians in biblical doctrine. Up until that point, every time he preached, people would weep loudly over their sin and need for Jesus. But David wanted them to grow in their knowledge of the Savior as well.

From that day forward, David began catechizing the Indians—asking them the questions stated in the Westminster Shorter Catechism and teaching them the answers. To his great surprise and joy, the new-found knowledge translated into an even greater heartfelt love for God and his work of redemption in Christ Jesus. Catechizing became part and parcel of Brainerd's ministry, usually as a follow-up to his preaching.

When he was not feeling too sick, he would visit his Indian friends in Crossweeksung, walking from one cottage to the next. He prayed with his people, taught his people, catechized his people, but most of all, he loved his people.

On Friday, January 31st, David's labors at recruiting a new schoolmaster to start an English school among the Crossweeksung Indians came to fruition. Ebenezer Hayward came to the village to be the new schoolmaster and to teach classes to adults and students alike. The people welcomed him with open arms. The very next day he held his first class. A crowd of thirty children and a score of teenagers attended.

It seemed as though the whole of Brainerd's ministry among the Indians at Crossweeksung brought forth spiritual fruit and God was blessing the labors of preaching and teaching. David preached throughout the week and, despite his ongoing sickness and fever, continued to pray and counsel men and women in how they ought to live out the faith they now professed.

Some men, who were known to be drunkards and murderers, now treated others with love and kindness. Women who had practiced witchcraft and idolatry, now praised Jesus as their only Savior and Lord. Several married couples who had previously separated and started living with somebody other than their spouse, now confessed their sin and reunited with their original mate in love and harmony. Family prayers became a regular feature of the Indian Christians as well as the honoring of the Lord's Day.

Adults and children continued to be educated in the new-found school and after only four-and-a-half months, many were reading the Psalms on their own. In addition, David continued to baptize new converts and catechize whole families at a time. The seeds of the gospel that David had planted and watered began to grow in great numbers.

However, despite all of the Christian growth, David observed among his congregation, challenges persisted. First, many Indians witnessed ungodly and immoral behavior among white settlers and didn't trust David's gospel message. "If that was the Christian way," they would tell him, "we don't want it!"

A second challenge, when encountering new Indians, was a fear that somehow David was tricking them in order to make them slaves. Some suspected that he would draw them with kindness only to trap them into serving the white settlers.

Third, most Indians held to a religious belief in worshiping a plurality of gods and different animals. They believed that the gods communicated to them through various creatures and would frequently offer sacrifices to these invisible powers. Witchdoctors seemed to have some control and power over invisible forces and were very influential among the various Indian tribes that David encountered. Under his ministry, God saved several of these witchdoctors, called "powwows" and brought about great gospel change in their lives.

A fourth challenge presented to David was the difficulty over translating various English words into whatever native language he came upon. For example, terms such as: "Savior, sinner, justice, faith, repentance, adoption, grace, glory, and heaven," didn't exist in the natives' languages. He had to formulate new words and use parts of their words to describe these biblical truths.

However, through these challenges and hardships God was pleased to shape David and to teach him to trust in his goodwill more. He had to trust that God's grace was sufficient for him. He had to trust that he would never be forsaken because Jesus was forsaken on his behalf. It always came back to the gospel. David showed patience toward the Indians because God had shown patience toward him in his sin. He forgave the Indians when they wronged him because God had forgiven him. David loved the Indians because God had first loved him. Jesus was the centerpiece of David's entire life to the point that, "to live is Christ and to die is gain" (Philippians 1:21).

* * *

English settlers had been moving into the Crossweeksung area, slowly swindling the Indians out of their lands. By March 1746, several Crossweeksung Indians traveled to an area fifteen miles northeast to clear some new land for a permanent settlement. The new site was located just outside of a town called Cranberry and situated at the head of a creek.

In May, the village packed up and moved, Brainerd following behind and arriving on May 3rd. At times, David felt that these Indians were more "his" people than the English and often held disdain for how many of the English treated his new Indian friends. In fact, when he encountered new natives, many would refuse to listen to him about the truths of Christianity because they had been turned off by the poor behavior and sinful practices of other so-called "Christian" white men.

Toward the end of May, a severe fever confined David to his straw cot. He was hardly able to hold down any food, causing his body to become very weak and frail. On top of that, the chest pain and the coughing of blood increased to new levels to the point that David loathed his very living.

Without a home and plagued with sickness, he opened his journal up on May 22nd and began to write:

"And it appears just right that I should be destitute of house and home, and many comforts of life which I rejoiced to see other of God's people enjoy. I rejoice to be a pilgrim or hermit in the wilderness, to my dying moment, if I might thereby promote the blessed interest of the great Redeemer."

He was certainly a pilgrim, passing through this world to the next. And though he had faced great danger, much suffering, and continued sickness, he was resolved to spend each moment, each thought, in service of King Jesus.

On Tuesday, August 12th, David set out with six fellow Indians from Cranberry for another mission trip to the Susquehanna. Not wanting to travel over the mountains and through the thick wilderness, he took a longer route through Philadelphia and arrived at a lower point on the Susquehanna River than where he had traveled before.

He and his companions—whom David brought along as a "witness" to the miraculous work of God in their lives—trekked up the river toward Shamokin, the large Indian camp that controlled much of the Susquehanna region. They couldn't find even a small cottage to sleep in and so nestled in some leaves on the bank of the river. That night, a huge thunderstorm swept through the gorge and drenched the shivering band of Christian brothers. They tried everything to protect themselves from the driving wind and rain, but it was no use. The storm seemed to not only pummel their bodies, but their souls as well.

When morning broke, he took out his journal and wrote of the hard night of little sleep: "Having lain in a cold sweat all night, I coughed much bloody matter this morning, and am under great disorder of body." The storm caused David's health to take a serious and rapid decline. Nevertheless, drenched to their bones, they continued on and reached Shamokin on the 23rd.

A great crowd of Indians—many of whom David recognized from previous trips—formed around the missionary as he preached of the love of God in sending his only Son to die in our place as a payment for our many sins. The Indians responded with great emotion and tears, wanting this forgiveness and salvation that David preached of.

After he had finished, he spent the remainder of the day and the next teaching the people in their homes and praying for many others individually. But the ministry had taken a toll on his body. The following day he was again coughing and spitting blood and felt very weak. He knew he needed to get back to his cottage in Cranberry and so set out with his traveling companions, hoping to live long enough to bring word to "his" people the good news of the Susquehanna journey.

By God's good grace, he arrived back at the Cranberry settlement on Saturday, September 20th. The next day, he preached sitting in a chair because he was too weak to stand. His fever and his coughs continued to worsen through that day and evening. He continued in this state of illness, to a greater and lesser measure, through the beginning of November. When he was able, he preached. When he was too sick, he stayed in bed.

Finally, on November 2nd, he wrote in his journal a very hard, but meaningful entry:

"Being now in so weak and low a state that I was utterly incapable of performing my work, and having little hope of recovery, I thought it my duty to take a lengthy journey into New England and to divert myself among my friends whom I had not now seen for a long time."

Before leaving his people, he gathered enough strength to visit them in their homes, encouraging them in the faith. He gave one final farewell speech, attended by many tears from the Indians. Many, no doubt knowing his illness, wondered if they would ever see him again.

That Glorious Day!

Winter 1746-7

It was a beautiful November day—crisp air and a fresh blanket of crunchy leaves covered the road from Cranberry to Elizabethtown. Despite the cool temperature, the clear blue sky and bright morning sun warmed the land and David's heart as he made his way to the home of Jonathan Dickinson.

He continued to think about and pray for his people at Cranberry, asking God to provide another minister to shepherd and care for their souls. He wanted them to keep growing and learning the truths of the glorious gospel of Jesus Christ.

Although he felt great love and a great desire to continue to watch over his flock in Cranberry, his chronic illness made his previous pace of ministry nearly impossible. When he arrived in Elizabethtown on November 4th, he was immediately struck by a high fever and confined to an upstairs bedroom in Dickenson's home. While in bed, he continued to write letters to friends and other ministers and made an effort to keep up his journal writing.

"Enabled to intercede with God for my dear congregation, very often for every family and every person in particular; and this a great comfort to me!"

Over the next five months, David remained in Elizabethtown—going in and out of varying degrees of illness and trying his best to minister to his visitors as well as people in Dickenson's own congregation.

Then on Friday, April 10th, David received a most welcome surprise. His brother, John, rode to Elizabethtown to talk with David about his missionary labors among the Indians at Crossweeksung and their move to the Cranberry settlement. Although David was extremely frail and weak, he rejoiced to talk with his brother and hear of his desire to enter into full-time ministry among the Indians. John, a recent graduate of Yale, had approached the Scottish Society about serving with David's congregation in Cranberry during his brother's absence.

The following Monday, David assisted in examining John, along with other members of the Scottish society in areas of theology, Bible knowledge and practical Christian experience. The examiners—David included—unanimously approved John to take his brother's place. John left the next day for Cranberry.

Six days later, on April 20th, David turned twenty-nine years old and spent much of the day suffering from high fever and painful coughing—an unpleasant birthday! But he was refreshed to learn about a new development taking place in Dickenson's home: the beginning of a new college for young ministers of the gospel.

Over the past several months, Jonathan Dickenson and some of his colleagues had become convinced that they needed to start a new college to train progressive evangelical ministers for gospel ministry. Dickenson, who would become the first president of the new college, had sympathy for Brainerd after his expulsion from Yale and that Yale didn't give Brainerd a degree.

The expulsion of David from Yale proved to Dickenson and his fellow ministers that a new college needed to be established for people like Brainerd and so they charted the College of New Jersey, known today as Princeton University. Several of the college's instructors noted that if it had not been for the harsh treatment David received at Yale, Princeton would not have been created.

During the following weeks, David's health actually began to improve and he was able to walk outside and even ride short distances on his horse. Thinking of his time at Yale and thankful for the advice of Jonathan Edwards to made amends with Yale's officials, he decided to visit Edwards in Northampton, Massachusetts, about 130 miles northeast of Elizabethtown.

He arrived at Edward's home unannounced on May 28th, 1747, feeling very weak again, though delighted to spend some quality time with the famous preacher. Edwards, for his part, was overjoyed to have the young missionary in his home for he had read David's report of his preaching and ministry along the Forks of the Delaware, the Susquehanna River, and his recent mission among the Crossweeksung Indians. When Brainerd showed up on his doorstep, Edwards was thrilled to hear of all his ministry labors first-hand.

* * *

"Is there not anything we can do, Doctor Mather?" Edwards asked outside of Brainerd's bedroom.

The older gentleman looked down at his medical bag, taking a deep breath. "I'm sorry, Jonathan. It appears that he has fluid-filled pockets on his lungs, which build and burst, causing extreme pain in his chest. There is nothing I can do and—," he paused to look back into Brainerd's bedroom, "I'm afraid he isn't going to be with us much longer. I'm sorry."

With that, the doctor walked down the staircase and out the front door, leaving Edwards very concerned about his missionary patient. He knew he needed to tell David everything, though wasn't exactly sure how he was going to take the hard news. Offering up a quick prayer, Jonathan entered the room.

The opening door seemed to startle David, who had drifted into a deep sleep while Doctor Mather and Edwards talked. "Oh, good sir, did the doctor leave already?" Brainerd said, trying to sit up slightly in his bed.

Jonathan grabbed a small wooden chair and sat down beside the bed. "Yes, he did. David, you probably are aware of your condition, but I need to tell you what the doctor told me."

David leaned forward a little and looked at Jonathan with a resolve to face anything he might say.

"Doctor Mather said that your ailments do not look as if they will improve. He wants you to get some rest, but know that he doesn't expect you to return to full health."

"Mr. Edwards, I am willing and ready to be in heaven with my Lord. Countless times I have desired this, but God has kept me here for a purpose—to make his wonderful gospel of Jesus known to the world. I am ready to die, whenever that day may come."

Feeling a little better the next day and able to ride, he wanted to travel to Boston in order to visit some ministerial friends. Edwards wasn't too fond of the idea, due to his poor health, but agreed and asked his seventeen-year-old daughter—Jerusha—to accompany him and take care of him along the way.

Jerusha was Edwards' second oldest daughter and had been giving care to David while at the Edwards' household. She was a delightfully joyful young woman who had a love for serving David. She greatly admired his zeal and courage in ministering among the Indians. She and David became very good friends and he became deeply grateful for her loving support and care.

The two of them rode to Boston, arriving on June 13th. They stayed in the home of a prominent Christian merchant named Edward Bromfield. The following week, David suddenly fell into the worst sickness of his life. Struck with a high fever, chest pain, and persistently coughing up blood, he was fairly certain this would be his final week.

Jerusha wrote home of David's condition:

"Doctor Pynchon says he has no hopes of his life; nor does he think it likely he will ever come out of the chamber, though he says he may be able to come to Northampton. He is extremely weak and very fair, expecting every day will be his last. He has hardly vigor enough to draw his breath. One can scarcely tell, at times, if he is alive or not."

Over a period of several weeks, however, and to everyone's great surprise, his health steadily improved. He actually began to engage in ministry as much as possible—writing letters, editing books, and keeping a steady output of journal writing.

In fact, on one occasion in mid July, he held a semi-public debate over a false doctrine called antinomianism with a brilliant young man named Andrew Croswell. Croswell taught that, since we are fully forgiven and accepted before God, then we can lead a life of sin because it makes God look more gracious. This was the basic premise of antinomianism. To this, David responded with a resounding, "No!" It was true that we are fully forgiven and accepted by God based on the work of Christ, but being now forgiven *frees* us to serve him and others with love and faith. While we are saved "by faith alone," faith never comes alone—it is always evidenced by good works.

Israel Brainerd, David's brother, also visited him while in Boston and they had opportunity to enjoy Christian and family fellowship. However, Israel brought sad news. Their younger sister, whose name was also Jerusha, had recently fallen ill and died at Haddam. Though David was saddened by the news, he was also comforted by the expectation that he would soon be reunited with her in heaven.

With his health continuing to improve for the time being, he thought it best to make one last travel back to Northampton where he could be taken care of by Jerusha and the Edwards' family. After bidding farewell to his friends in Boston, he, his brother, Israel and Jerusha rode to Northampton, arriving on July 25th. For the next few weeks, David continued to do some writing and ministry around the greater Northampton area.

On Sunday, August 16th, David had enough strength to attend Edwards' church service for what would end up being his last Sunday worship experience. That following Thursday, David, suffering from a new wave of exhaustion and fever, could no longer manage going up and down the stairs to his bedroom at Jonathan's home. The family decided to set up a room for him downstairs and devoted themselves to taking care of David—especially Jerusha.

* * *

"Mr Brainerd, there's somebody here to see you!" Jerusha said with restrained excitement.

David immediately tried to sit up, propping himself upon on his pillow. "Who is it?"

All of the sudden, Jerusha went out of the room and in walked a tall, but rather dirty young man.

"John!" David said almost shouting with joy, quickly cut short by a painful cough.

"Hello, my brother. I received word that you were very ill and wanted to see you again and to encourage you with good news."

David motioned to a nearby wooden chair. "Please sit down and let us enjoy some good conversation. I want to hear of this news, that my soul may be filled with delight in what the Lord is doing through your ministry."

"David, God is certainly providing a steady increase and harvest of your planting and watering of the gospel at Cranberry." John scooted his chair a bit closer and leaned toward the bed. "Thirty new Indians have come to the settlement since your departure and all of them seem convinced of the truth of the Christian religion!"

"That is wonderful, John! Praise God!"

"Moreover, I found some of your old journals and thought you might want to have them—perhaps so that you could read through some of them for fun." He reached down and pulled out several well-worn leather journals and handed them to David.

"I almost forgot about these." He opened the cover of one of them and remembered the exact time and place of penning the words. "Thank you, John. You do not know how much this means to me—that you are here to visit and tell of your labors among my people at Cranberry."

"Of course, David. You are a great example of faith and courage and I look up to you, not only as my older brother, but as a model of Christian character, of humility and of having a love for the lost."

The two of them spent the evening talking about all that had happened at the mission over the summer. The next day, John had to leave to take care of some of the natives back in Cranberry, but promised to be back soon—knowing that David's health was slowly, but surely failing. After he left, David took out his current journal and began to write of his impressions of reading over his old entries:

"Lord's Day, September 6th. I began to read some of my private writings, which my brother brought me; and was considerably refreshed with what I met with in them. I could not but rejoice and bless God for what passed long ago, which without writing had been entirely lost."

Amazingly, he was so spiritually refreshed after reading his own journals, that he decided—at the urging of some close friends—to edit them and give them to Jonathan Edwards for publishing. "Others," he thought, "might benefit from reading these."

A couple of weeks later, on September 19th, David tried to get up and walk around his bedroom during the late afternoon, hoping to feel some ease from the pain in his chest. While taking a few steps, he immediately felt a tremendous spiritual attack from Satan.

"You are a dirty, sinful creature, not fit for heaven. God will not accept you for you are too unworthy and depraved!" he thought.

But in that moment, even after feeling much dejection and melancholy during his years in missionary labors, he was surprised to find his heart and mind fixated on gospel truth:

"I know I am unworthy," he thought to himself. "But what of it? For there stands in my place One who calls me his own and wraps a robe of perfect righteousness around me. I exalt in my Savior and triumph in his finished work on my behalf. He is my great righteousness and nobody and nothing can snatch me from his hand!"

With that, his body became overwhelmed with sickness and he collapsed onto his bed. Jerusha heard him fall and ran into the room. "Mr Brainerd," she said rushing to straighten him out. She quickly plunged a nearby rag into a bowl of cool water and began dabbing his forehead.

"I am sorry to see you in such misery, Mr. Brainerd."

Barely able to breathe through the intense pain, he found her hand with his and held it as if to say "thank you". Jerusha was his constant caretaker and friend. Unfortunately, she too began to feel weak and sick—having similar pains and fever. But she didn't let this be known to David. She wanted to be a strong source of continual comfort and rest for her ailing patient.

A little over a week later, he pulled out his journal for what would be his last entry, and began to write:

"Friday, October 2nd. My soul was this day, at turns, sweetly set on God: I long to be with him that I might behold his glory. I felt sweetly disposed to commit all to him, even my dearest friends, my dearest flock, and my absent brother, John, and all my concerns for time and eternity. Oh, that his kingdom might come in the world; that they might all love and glorify him for what he is in himself. Oh, come, Lord Jesus, come quickly! Amen."

David's brother, John, finally came back the following Wednesday and the two continued their conversation about John's ministry among David's "people" in Cranberry. They talked all day Thursday, interrupted from time to time with violent coughs and grimacing pain.

Late on Thursday evening, the two began talking of the joys of heaven and of their desire to see the expansion of Christ's kingdom here on earth. Indeed, it was for this very purpose that David had labored for these many years. He enjoyed hearing about John's passion and excitement over God's miraculous work in the hearts of the natives. The more that John shared, the more David's heart melted with gladness. And the more his heart melted with gladness, the more his body weakened.

Finally, around six in the morning on Friday, October 9th, 1747, David's eyes became fixed and he passed from this life into the next—from this troubled world into his heavenly home. He was finally with his blessed Savior, Jesus, and beheld him face to face. To many, it was a sad day to lose such a faithful man of God. But to David, the day couldn't have been more glorious.

Epilogue and Influence

Jonathan Edwards officiated Brainerd's funeral the following Monday, October 12th at his church in Northampton, preaching from 2 Corinthians 5:8. He was buried in the Northampton churchyard and a great crowd of many godly ministers and congregants attended the service.

It was with great sadness, though by divine appointment, that David's brother, Israel, fell ill and died several months later. In addition, Jerusha—David's faithful companion and sweet caretaker in the Edwards' home—also passed away due to illness on February 14th, 1748. She was buried in the same churchyard, immediately next to Brainerd.

David's brother, John, continued serving and ministering to the Indians until his death in 1781, at age sixty-one. Over those years, he saw his native congregation grow both spiritually and numerically. Indeed, John inherited the missionary groundwork laid by David at Crossweeksung and at Cranberry.

Jonathan Edwards took Brainerd's journals, edited them, and published them under the title, *The Life of David Brainerd*, in 1749. It was the first full-length missionary biography ever written and eventually became the most popular of all of Edward's many works.

The fact that David's journals and life story has had an influence since his death in October 1747 is an understatement. Countless men and women have read his journal and been inspired by his selfless life, his steady resolve, and his personal love for God. People like John Wesley, William Carey, Robert Murray McCheyne, and Jim Elliot have all paid their respect to Brainerd.

May many more thousands be drawn to the love of God and the saving grace of Jesus Christ through the life witness and ministry of the young missionary to the Native Americans.

Thinking Further Topics

Chapter 1– Mystery in the Making

Have you ever baked a cake or helped prepare a dinner for your family before? I remember making my first set of cupcakes with my mother when I was ten years old. We mixed up all the ingredients and then put the batter into small paper cups (licking the spoon between each new cup!). We put the tray into the oven and then waited. And we waited some more. I didn't know how they were going to turn out, but I knew they would be good because my mom was overseeing the whole project!

The Apostle Paul tells us in the book of Romans that all things work together for good, for those who love God and are called according to his purpose (Rom. 8:28). Sometimes waiting is hard to do. But God promises us that all things work out according to his plan and purpose. What a great comfort to know that God is in control even when circumstances seem difficult or mysterious. When you find yourself anxious about the future, rest in the knowledge that God has a plan for your life and that he calls you to love and trust him every day!

Chapter 2 – Hazed and Confused

When David was a teenager, he read through the Bible twice in one year. The Bible is a long book. Actually, it is a collection of sixty-six books that all point to Jesus Christ—thirty-nine in the Old Testament and twenty-seven in the New Testament. The unique thing about the Bible is that it is God's Word, which means that, while the words contained were written by human authors, the true author was God. He inspired the text of the Bible by the Holy Spirit to reveal his character, his promises, and the gospel of Jesus Christ to us.

I don't know if you have ever taken time to study the Bible, but there is nothing better for your heart and soul. Psalm 119:105 says, "Thy word is a lamp unto my feet and a light unto my path." The Bible holds within it tremendous and wonderful treasures of peace, comfort, joy, and truth about our relationship with God through his Son, Christ Jesus. You might want to begin in the book of the Gospel of John and read through the exciting life of Jesus. Wherever your heart may be, let it find rest in the knowledge of the good news of Christ, found in the pages of God's Word.

Chapter 3 – Expelled!

Sometimes it's hard to resist the temptation to be critical about someone behind their back, especially if you find yourself in a group of friends who are already taking part. On the other hand, it is very painful when others are being critical about you. There is an old saying that goes, "Sticks and stones may break my bones, but words will never hurt." How untrue! Words do hurt. I don't know if you've ever been really hurt by what a friend or a family member has said to you or about you, but it can be very painful.

1 Thessalonians 5:11 says that we are to build one another up. That means that we should encourage each other by speaking kind words and serving each other's needs. It means being humble and not trying to boast of your accomplishments and abilities at another's expense. When you criticise somebody, you are criticising a fellow human being who has been created in the image of God. That person, whether he or she is a friend or a classmate, was created for a relationship with God. So go, and build up that person and encourage him or her to be reconciled to God through Jesus Christ!

Chapter 4 – A Call in the Woods

You might not have ever heard of the Westminster Shorter Catechism, but David Brainerd knew it well. The Catechism was written in the 1640s at Westminster Abbey in London. It was designed to help train children in the doctrines and truths of the Christian faith. As David prepared to preach the gospel, he was examined in areas of theology, Bible knowledge, and his Christian experience. He learned the Catechism together with a Larger Catechism and the Westminster Confession of Faith.

But the first question of the Shorter Catechism is very important and asks, "What is the chief end of man?" Answer: "The chief end of man is to glorify God and to enjoy him forever." The amazing thing about this answer is that we are to enjoy God! Christianity isn't a cold, heartless religion, but a joyful, delight-filled, relationship with a loving and holy God. Our hearts are to long for God "as a deer panteth for water brooks" (Psalm 42:1). Psalm 90:14 says, "O satisfy us early with thy mercy, that we may rejoice and be glad all our days." Let your soul find great enjoyment and delight in the steadfast love of God!

Chapter 5 – The Traveling Preacher

David Brainerd felt compelled to tell the native Indians about the gospel of Jesus Christ. He believed it was his calling in life—that he was to be a missionary. If you are a Christian reading this, you might never experience that particular call from God. But God does call you to share your faith with unbelievers, with gentleness and respect. All too often, Christians who try to convince unbelievers of the truths do it in a way that is confrontational. Peter told the early Christians to "be ready always to give an answer to every man that asketh you for a reason of the hope that is in you with meekness and fear" (1 Peter 3:15). In other words, we should be ready to share our faith and the reason for the hope we have in the gospel of Jesus Christ, but we should do so with humility and gentleness. Jesus told his followers to go into all the world and make disciples of him (Matthew 28:19). Have you had the opportunity to share the gospel with somebody recently? Pray and ask God to bring somebody into your life to whom you could give the reason for the hope you have in Christ Jesus.

Chapter 6 – A Hard Life Among the Indians

We often become more thankful for the things we have when, for a season, they are gone. When I was growing up, I used to go camping with my friends. I loved being out in the woods on a cool autumn evening, roasting some marshmallows over a fire and looking at the grand display of the evening stars. Few things are better, until it's time to go to sleep and you don't have a bed! All of the sudden, I would wish for my comfy bed that I had back home, and not the hard ground underneath my sleeping bag.

David Brainerd had a very difficult life—sleeping on a thin layer of straw, eating boiled corn for every meal and not knowing if he would survive the next cold winter. He was grateful for the little things that we so often take for granted. But we should be thankful for all that God gives us. Colossians 1:15 says that we are to be thankful, especially for the salvation that God has worked in our hearts. While we should never forget to be grateful for the material blessings in life, we should be even more grateful for the good news of the gospel!

Chapter 7 – A New Call to the Frontier!

Can you think of the farthest place you have ever been from home? It might have been a vacation or to see a relative. I remember traveling to the country of Cambodia to preach the gospel to a cluster of churches. It took nearly forty hours of travel time to get from the southern portion of the United States to a remote village in eastern Cambodia. It was the longest journey I had ever taken.

Believe it or not, you and I are on a journey even as you read this. We are actually pilgrims passing through this world onto the next. This world is not our true home. Our home is with Jesus in heaven, but we are here to see the progress and joy of others in him (Philippians 1:25). Jesus told his disciples in John 14:3, "If I go and prepare a place for you, I will come again, and receive you unto myself, that where I am, there ye may be also." God is calling each of us heavenward. Jesus will come back again and judge the living and the dead. Are you ready? Have you put your faith and trust in Jesus Christ as your Savior? Is he Lord of your life? Take joy in the knowledge that we will some day be in our true home, even if the present journey is long and difficult.

Chapter 8 – The Ground Breaks Open

Working a garden is no easy task. The tilling, planting, protecting, and picking can all take their toll on the gardener. The sun is often relentless and the days are long, but the reward of fresh fruit and vegetables makes the hard work worth it.

Writing in 1 Corinthians 3:7, Paul explains how the "fruit" of salvation comes from planting and watering the gospel. He writes, "So then neither he that planteth any thing, neither he that watereth; but God that giveth the increase." Our task is to plant and water the gospel, which means to be faithful to God in obedience to his Word. There are some people who hear the gospel message day in and day out for years and then, one day, God gives the growth in the heart and they are saved.

If this has happened in your heart, stop and thank God for saving you. Sometimes, we want to take the credit for our salvation or we want to believe that our good works earn our salvation. But the Bible is clear to say that our faith is a gift—indeed, all of salvation is a gift—so that we would not boast. Let us plant and water the gospel and trust God to cause our faith to grow.

Chapter 9 – Pressing On Toward Exhaustion

David Brainerd grew tired of laboring alone. He wanted Christian companionship. He wanted somebody to share his struggles with, his fears with and his joys with. Friends are wonderful gifts from God. True friends know a lot about you— even things you may not want them to know— and will love you anyway! By God's grace, he has provided a community of people who surround us with love, support, accountability, and service: the church.

In Ephesians chapter four, Paul calls the church the "body of Christ". We are all different members of the body, working together for a common goal of giving glory to God. One of the ways we do that is through a grace-centered community. We are to pray for one another, listen to one another, study God's Word together, worship together, love one another and hold each other accountable. The body of Christ is a family and a gift to you. Are you involved in a local church? If not, search out a gospel-driven, Bible-believing church to attend and to get plugged into. May it be a source of great delight and growth in your Christian life!

Chapter 10 – A Love for My People

Toward the end of his life, David Brainerd began to experience intense internal pain from his tuberculosis.

He frequently coughed up blood and breathing became very burdensome. But while his pain grew, so did his love for his Indian people. The interesting thing about his situation was that he literally gave his life to serve and advance the gospel among them.

"But God commendeth his love toward us, in that, while we were yet sinners, Christ died for us" (Romans 5:8). Jesus experienced unbearable suffering. He was whipped almost to the point of death. He was beaten and ridiculed. And finally, he was stretched out on a cross to suffer and die. But what those Romans didn't know was that Jesus' death was "plan A". He gave up his life so that you and I might live. He was forsaken by God so that you and I would never be. Our sin was placed upon his shoulders and he paid for it all and, in return, he gave us his perfect record of righteousness. When God looks upon you, believer, he sees the righteousness of his Son and now declares you, "not guilty!" Praise God for loving us as his people even while we were sinners.

Chapter 11 – That Glorious Day!

All of us have had moments of great fear when we were absolutely afraid of something or somebody. When I was eight years old, I went caving with my father. We took flashlights, a climbing rope and a couple of bottles of water into a deep cave in the mountains of Tennessee. After about an hour, I had no clue where we were and I began to get very scared. I began to think about my situation—being underground with no food and I felt totally lost. But then I realized that my dad knew exactly where we were and how to get out. Although I didn't have a clue, he did and that gave me great comfort!

When Jesus left this earth and ascended into heaven, he sent the Holy Spirit to be our guide and our protector. In fact, Ephesians 1:13 says that we are "sealed with the Holy Spirit". This means that, when we feel scared or when we may even doubt our salvation, we should trust the fact that God has sealed us by his Spirit and he will lead us out of this worldly cave in victory over death and hell forever. That, my friend, will be a glorious day!

David Brainerd
Timeline

1718   David Brainerd born in Haddam, Connecticut.
New Orleans is founded on the Mississippi River.

1719   *Robinson Crusoe* by Daniel Defoe is published.

1721   Smallpox vaccination first administered.

1724   Gabriel Fahrenheit invents the first mercury thermometer.

1727   David Brainerd's father dies.
King George II ascends the English throne.
Brazil plants its first coffee.

1732   David Brainerd's mother dies, and he goes to live with an older sister.

1736   Russia and Austria at war with Turkey.
Natural rubber discovered in the rain forests of Peru.

1737   David Brainerd inherits family farm near Durham.

1739   David Brainerd's conversion to Christianity.
Enrolls at Yale to prepare for ministry.
England declares war on Spain.
The Great Awakening begins.

1741   David Brainerd is expelled from Yale for making a negative comment about one of Yale's tutors.

1742   David Brainerd is licensed to preach by a group of "New Light" ministers.
Approved by the Scottish Society to embark on missionary work among the native Indians

1742   First indoor swimming pool opens in London.

1743	David Brainerd began work among the Indians at Kaunaumeek.
	David makes amends with Yale officials.
	Handel's Oratoria "Messiah" has its London premiere.
1744	David Brainerd arrives at the Forks of the Delaware to begin missionary work among the local native Indians; ordained to gospel ministry.
	Makes first journey to the Susquehanna River to evangelize various native tribes.
1745	Makes first journey to Crossweeksung to preach.
	Revival breaks out at Crossweeksung through Brainerd's preaching; then at Forks of the Delaware.
1746	Starts a school among the Crossweeksung Indians.
	Relocates with Crossweeksung Indians to new settlement near Cranberry.
1747	Leaves Cranberry for the last time; travels to Elizabethtown.
	John Brainerd takes David's place among the Cranberry settlement.
	David arrives at Jonathan Edwards' home; becomes very ill and looked after by Edwards' daughter, Jerusha.
	Dies in the home of Jonathan Edwards.

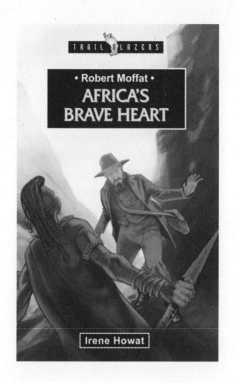

Robert Moffat, Africa's Brave Heart
by Irene Howat
ISBN 978-1-84550-715-2

The story of a Scottish minister and his wife in Africa
– the precursors to David Livingstone. With a sword,
a shovel, a Bible, and great courage, Robert used the
skills he had learned growing up in a Scottish village
to translate the Bible into Tswana and to share God's
love with Africa.

OTHER BOOKS IN THE
TRAILBLAZER SERIES

The Adventures Series
An ideal series to collect

Have you ever wanted to visit the rainforest? Have you ever longed to sail down the Amazon river? Would you just love to go on Safari in Africa? Well, these books can help you imagine that you are actually there.

Pioneer missionaries retell their amazing adventures and encounters with animals and nature. In the Amazon you will discover tree frogs, piranha fish and electric eels. In the rainforest you will be amazed at the armadillo and the toucan. In the blistering heat of the African Savannah you will come across lions and elephants and hyenas. And you will discover how God is at work in these amazing environments.

Rocky Mountain Adventures by Betty Swinford
ISBN 978-1-85792-962-1

CHRISTIAN FOCUS PUBLICATIONS

Christian Focus | Christian Heritage | CF4K | Mentor

Christian Focus Publications publishes books for adults and children under its four main imprints: Christian Focus, CF4K, Mentor and Christian Heritage. Our books reflect our conviction that God's Word is reliable and Jesus is the way to know him, and live for ever with him.

Our children's publication list includes a Sunday School curriculum that covers pre-school to early teens, and puzzle and activity books. We also publish personal and family devotional titles, biographies and inspirational stories that children will love.

If you are looking for quality Bible teaching for children then we have an excellent range of Bible stories and age-specific theological books.

From pre-school board books to teenage apologetics, we have it covered!

Find us at our web page:
www.christianfocus.com

CF4•K
Because you're never
too young to know Jesus